This Minute Matters

The Essence of Presence

Deborah LeBlanc, CCHt CAHA

Copyright © 2024 Deborah LeBlanc
All rights reserved.

Table of Contents

	Introduction	5
1	**Be There**	9
	Mindfulness Exercise: A Quick Taste of Intentional Living	10
	Mindfulness Exercise: The Detective	13
	Mindfulness and the Science behind It	17
2	**Listen to Laughter and Smell the Roses**	20
	Mindfulness Exercise: Creating a Colorful Calendar as a Visual Aid for Your "Prime Times"	22
	Mindfulness Exercise: Making a Morning Meditation Box	25
	Picking Your Perfect Moments and Exploiting Sensory Loopholes	29
	Evolving Your Process—Switching Things up to Keep Your Moments More Memorable	35
3	**Cook with Love**	40
	A Mindful Practice That Pays Delectable Dividends at the End!	40
	Why Cooking from Scratch Is the Way to Go—The Benefits of Taking Your Time	41

	Cooking from Scratch—A Quick Crash Course to Get You Started	43
	Remember FASHion—Fat, Acid, Salt, Heat—It's on NOW!	46
	Substitutions—Learn Them and Play with Them	47
	Simple Recipes You Can Make from Scratch	48
	Bonus Mindfulness Exercise: Miracle Fruit!	66
4	**Act with Kindness**	**68**
	How Little Things Can Lighten Up Your Entire Day	68
	Little Acts of Kindness Make Big Waves—And Science Backs This Up	72
	Acts of Kindness Actually Reduce Daily Stress and Can Help Stop Dangerous Cycles	73
5	**Forgive and Let Go**	**92**
	The Importance of Forgiveness	93
	How Resentments Steal Your Time Away	96
	Forgiveness Is a Gift to Yourself: Learning How to Let Go	97
	Mindfulness Exercise: Two Handles Meditation	99
	Mindfulness Exercise: Putting Critics in Their Place	102
	Mindfulness Exercise: I Am Not the One You Harmed	106
Conclusion		**111**
Bibliography		**114**

Introduction

There's a quote that I've always liked that comes from a Stoic philosopher named Seneca, who died way back in 65 AD. It goes like this:

"The greatest obstacle to living is expectancy, which hangs upon tomorrow and loses today."[1]

The closest thing that we have to that quote today is the old chestnut "A watched pot never boils," which communicates essentially the same thing—stop stretching out time in the wrong areas of your life because you've got more important things to do!

Both quotes hit the nail on the head in our modern lives. As card-carrying members of the rat race, we spend most of our precious time in an enormous rush through the present in order to secure a murky concept we call our "future."

The alarm goes off, and we rush out of bed to shower (or to feed the kids and pets and then shower), followed by a hasty breakfast of our own before embarking outside to fight other rat racers rushing to work in traffic.

---

[1] Seneca, *On the Shortness of Life: Life Is Long If You Know How to Use It*, trans. C. D. N. Costa (New York: Penguin Books, 2005).

Once in the office, we'll rush some more as our day passes, and we keep glancing at the clock until we're "free," only to hurry home and have our personal time spoiled—because we've already got our eyes on the upcoming weekend.

The second verse is the same as the first: Work, sleep, rinse, repeat. When does life start slowing down?

The thing is that every one of us has a lot more freedom than we realize and that "watched pot" adage actually gives us a hint on how to get it.

Consider this—you already know that looking at the coffee pot or tea kettle makes those seconds seem like hours, so why can't you simply apply that same principle to the moments that YOU want to stretch out?

You can—and you should!

According to United Nations projections, as of 2024 folks living in the United States have a life expectancy of 79.25 years. If you break that down into minutes, it's over forty million (41,653,800 to be precise), and each and every one of those minutes can be a gift to you or even become a priceless memory when you share them with people in your life.

It's all about knowing how to make all your moments into "watched pot" moments in a positive way, or to put it more elegantly, you need to learn the essence of presence.

Stopping yourself from rushing so that you can take a moment to notice what's around you is part of it, but there's a little more to it. You'll also need to actively assert yourself in the moment.

Think of it as "taking the reins" so that you can steer your time and start taking the scenic route rather than flying down the highway and missing everything along the way.

Don't believe that it works? Think about the most vivid of your memories, and you'll find that most of them reside in your childhood years. It makes sense—mindfulness is our default state as children—when there's possibly a diamond in every stone, and the threat of Mom or Dad calling you back home makes you appreciate every single second of your freedom.

In this book, I'm going to share some modern science and psychology techniques to help you build a solid framework to access that "default state of wonder" again. I'll divide up the chapters as follows and give you a little hint below of the lessons you'll learn to master in each:

- **Chapter 1—"Be There":** An exploration of how to be present in every moment by being intentional, as well as a primer on what science and modern studies say that mindfulness can do for your life.

- **Chapter 2—"Listen to Laughter and Smell the Roses":** On the importance of tackling time and milking every minute for everything it's worth.

- **Chapter 3—"Cook with Love":** Remember the smell of freshly baked bread at Grandma's house? We'll cover why adding taste to your time-bending toolbox is a MUST!

- **Chapter 4—"Act with Kindness":** A small kindness is like a pebble tossed in a still pond—it ripples out widely into the world around it, and it's a fine way to get more mileage out of those minutes.

- **Chapter 5—"Forgive and Let Go":** The past has already stolen its allotted time, and it's up to you to stop it from taking more than it's due. In this chapter, you'll find out how.

In each chapter, I include some exercises to help you to master the basic principles. You'll also find a bibliography in the back so that if you see a reference footnote to a book or a study that piques your interest, then you'll have all those references in one convenient place.

By the time we're done, you'll be well on your way to relearning that important life lesson that you knew instinctively so long ago.

Every minute is a treasure, and you shouldn't waste a single one!

Chapter One

Be There

Mastering your moments isn't just about slowing the world down so that you can appreciate the good things around you. That is an important part—after all, one of our biggest problems is ignoring everything but the clock—but once you've slowed things down, you could easily lose yourself in the minutia.

That's a great way to meditate properly and while I certainly recommend that you make a little time to do that, mindful moment mastery is going to also require that you take an active role.

The easiest way to remember it is a mnemonic device like this cute little rhyme: "Be there, be here, be mindful of your sphere."

This breaks down into three simple rules:

1. To "be there," you need to push the rat race and other external distractions away for the moment so that you can take in your surroundings properly. Imagine that this place is completely new to you, and you're trying to create a photo of it in your mind, but one that also includes your senses of touch, sound, taste, and scent to go with the sights.

2. To "be here," you need to take that inventory that you've just created of what's all around you at the moment and contemplate it like an artist looking at a junk pile that will soon become a powerful sculpture. Then you'll need to make that "minute sculpture."

3. To be "mindful of your sphere" just means to keep your consciousness confined to the immediate space around you—all those little things that are yours to experience and control. Aside from the physical components, the outside influences should be kept out as well. Don't worry about what the neighbors are doing or what might happen at work tomorrow—simply focus on the here and now and all the potentially wonderful things you can do with that.

What you're doing here is sowing the seeds of intentional living, and what this boils down to is best summed up as "Deciding to make your OWN choices instead of letting the people and the world around you make them for you."

It's something that gets easier with practice, and we'll start off small, but understand that the goal is the same—taking an inventory of what's around you and, this is the important part, deciding what to do with it NOW.

Mindfulness Exercise: A Quick Taste of Intentional Living

What You'll Need:

- 1 lemon

- a bowl of sugar or your favorite sweetener

- 1 drinking glass and one slightly larger plastic glass (or saucer that will fit over the top of your glass)

THIS MINUTE MATTERS: THE ESSENCE OF PRESENCE

- some ice
- 1 wooden kitchen spoon
- 1 kitchen knife
- a small amount of time when you won't be disturbed—half an hour is just about perfect!

How It's Done:

1. We'll start with a basic breathing exercise—don't worry, nothing fancy here—simply breathe in for a count of three, hold that breath in for a count of three, and then exhale for a count of three.

2. Close your eyes and breathe like this for a few moments until this breathing pattern feels natural, rather than forced, and then it's time to take your inventory of what's around you, starting with the sounds.

3. Are there sounds inside of the home or coming from outside? If you are in an apartment, do you hear the neighbors moving around? Don't strain; just let what's easily the apparent flow in and catalog it. For this exercise, you want to keep your awareness limited to a sphere of area immediately around you, and as you get a little practice, you can slowly widen that sphere and your own active awareness.

4. Once you're comfortable that you've created an "auditory catalog" of the sounds around you, then it's time to take your awareness to something more tactile. Pick something nearby to touch and contemplate for a moment—it could be anything—such as the leathery or velvety feel of the furniture upholstery, the

plush carpet at your feet, or the fine fabric of a garment you're wearing.

5. Take a moment to appreciate the textures around you and then open your eyes to catalog the sights. What colors and patterns pop out the most to you? Does any of the visual stimuli make you want to touch the item to see how it feels? Is the light in the room a little harsh or warm and mild?

6. Now that you've taken in an auditory, tactile, and visual inventory of the room, what about the scents and taste?

7. Here's where we get to flex our intentional living muscles a bit. Start off by opening the window to let in a little fresh air and take a moment to contemplate the scent—if it's pleasant, then keep the window open, but if the outside smells coming in are not to your liking, then close the window right away—you're in control, after all.

8. Next, go to your kitchen, and take your lemon off the counter or out of the fridge, and get your kitchen knife. Rinse the lemon and cut the nubs off the side, then cut the lemon into two halves and drop them into your glass.

9. Fill the glass halfway with water and smoosh the lemon halves with your wooden spoon, before adding a small handful of ice and a spoonful or three of sugar. Now cover the glass with your small saucer or slightly larger glass and give it a few shakes to mix and cool it.

10. Congratulations—you've just made quick a "carnival lemonade," and you're about to make a simple and delightful lasting moment that YOU created.

11. Take a good look at the color of your fresh lemonade and take a second to appreciate the feel of the cold glass in your hands. Take a sniff of the fresh, sweet and sour citrus inside, and tip it to your lips. Close your eyes first for maximum effect and then simply take your time to savor and enjoy it.

This is a very simple exercise but it literally gives you a taste of intentional living. I put in one more exercise for now before we move alone. Don't be surprised if you start seeing a few exercises waiting for you at the end of each chapter!

Mindfulness Exercise: The Detective

Sometimes you need to slow down the world around you in order to get your bearings, and you need to be sure that you aren't letting your brain run into that "blur" territory in your memory that comes from moving too fast.

In the exercise below, I'll give you a simple way to do this that you can practice on your own. By controlling your breathing and engaging all five of your senses individually, you can slow things down for a few moments, and it should be enough to get you calm and mindful to help you enjoy your day ahead—instead of simply letting your brain run on autopilot.

Let's take a look!

What You'll Need:

- You'll only need yourself—this meditation is self-contained and 100 percent portable. No props or assembly are required!

How It's Done:

1. Take a quick peek at the time, and then let's get started!

2. You'll want to center yourself with a quick breathing exercise first so that you'll be able to draw together the necessary focus for this exercise. You can use your favorite breathing exercise or do a basic three-three-three where you'll simply breathe in for three seconds, hold that breath for three seconds, and exhale it for three seconds. Repeat this until you don't have to count to maintain it and then we're ready to go!

3. We're going to put ourselves in a more mindful, observative state, much the way that they depict a detective's mind working on popular crime shows. We'll do this by engaging all five senses individually so that you can reset the autopilot mode in your mind and actively engage in sampling your surroundings for the rest of the day.

4. We'll start with sight—with a quick glance around the room, try to notice one thing that sticks out the most to you. It can be anything—If you're at work, it might be a coworker's awkward-colored sweater, low levels of water in the water cooler, or maybe one ceiling tile that looks off. If you're at home, it might be an out-of-place book, a particularly colorful plant, or even the dishes you forgot to do last night. Take a mental snapshot and visualize that detail off to the side in your mind.

5. Next, you want to hear a particular sound that is distinguishable from the rest. Maybe someone is using a copy machine nearby, or a coworker has a particularly distinctive laugh. If you're home, it could be a bird singing outside or the sounds of someone getting up in another part of the house. Capture that sound and stick it

off to the side with your "visual capture" component—you can see it as a sound wavelength, a ball of energy, or simply add the sound to the visual you've already separated.

6. Now we need a tactile component, and this is easy. You can feel the fabric of the clothing that you are wearing, touch a nearby piece of furniture, or even fish out your wallet like you're looking for something so that you can touch it and note how the texture feels to your fingers. Move that over to your mental collection on the side, visualizing it as a hand, or if you like, associate it with the visual component you already saved. You should be able to see it and feel it with the new texture in your mind—this is a good creative exercise on its own for abstract thought.

7. Locate a scent in your current environment that seems to stick out the most to you. Maybe there is a scent of coffee in the air or fresh paper. The air might smell a little stale in the room, or if you're at home and the window's open, it might be fresh. It may take a few moments, but if you breathe in lightly with your nose and take a moment to catalog your surroundings, the right scent will come to you, and you can file it to the side on its own or in a composite you're building of the five senses.

8. The final scent to stimulate is taste, and you can either note the current taste in your mouth or partake in a little coffee or another beverage or fish out a candy if you have some. If nothing is handy, run your tongue along your teeth for a moment and breathe in a little and out from your mouth and you'll notice a taste that you can set aside with the other captured sense-sample.

9. Now take a moment to review the samples you have set aside in your mind. Experience them individually first and then try to visualize experiencing them altogether by combining all the stimuli

into a new thing made out of many different ones. This will help to give you a creativity kick that you can use for the rest of the day, and you can end this mediation by promising yourself to take a little more time to take in your surroundings for the rest of the day.

10. Look at the time again and note how little time has passed—this is just a taste of what being more mindful of your surroundings can give to you!

The first few times that you do this will actually take a little longer, but with practice, you'll get very good at it. As an added bonus, you'll notice a lot more detail about places that you visit if you do this meditation often.

In turn, that tends to make your memory seem a lot more reliable, but really, all you are doing is taking an active role in your time. Think of it as "stopping to smell the roses" that you can use anywhere you like to help make sure that this minute matters!

Being in the moment isn't enough if you're simply slowing down and letting the world lead your focus. Instead, you need to get in the habit of actively taking an inventory of what is immediately in your sphere and, more importantly, what is in your control, and then making the decision to manipulate it to make the moment YOURS.

As we move through the chapters together, I'll give you more exercises that will help you to gradually extend that control so that you can maximize your moments and even share them with someone special. That way you won't be limited to making the most of your own moments but you will be also able to turn a little "ordinary time" into a priceless piece of nostalgia that you and your loved one can enjoy for the rest of your lives.

If you're worried that the exercise seems a bit simple, don't be—the goal here is to teach you to appreciate and exert your will on the world around you, just like you did as a child—and mindfulness is the way to do it.

For those of you out there who think mindfulness is kind of gimmicky, I wanted to share a little something that might interest you—studies have shown that mindfulness affects specific parts of your brain that can have very practical and profound effects on your life.

Mindfulness and the Science Behind It

When someone mentions the term "mindfulness," it can have a funny effect going around the room—some folks get excited and want to talk more about it, while others may adopt a neutral face or even a skeptical smirk.

That's because since mindfulness has gone mainstream, a lot of people tend to write it off as some sort of new-age fad, and that couldn't be further from the truth.

An article from *Psychology Today* written by Tim Lomas, PhD,[2] brings to light some of the history behind it, and it turns out that the term "mindfulness" dates all the way back to 1910. It's attributed to a Buddhist scholar by the name of T. W. Rhys Davids, who translated *Buddhist Suttas* into English[3] – where a *sutta* refers to a written "discourse of the Buddha." Davids originally used the term *sati* to describe what we all know as "mindfulness," and *sati* simply means "memory" or "retention" but is also associated with the core Buddhist lesson that one must "always remember to observe." Eventually, the scholar decided that the term "mindfulness" was a much better way to express this practice and one that would be much easier for readers to comprehend and use, so he introduced it in *Dialogues of the Buddha Volume 2*.[4]

---

[2] Tim Lomas, "Where Does the Word 'Mindfulness' Come From?," *Psychology Today*, March 16, 2016, https://www.psychologytoday.com/us/blog/finding-light-in-the-darkness/201603/where-does-the-word-mindfulness-come.

[3] *Buddhist Suttas*, trans. T. W. Rhys Davids (Oxford: Clarendon Press, 1881).

[4] *Dialogues of the Buddha Volume 2*, trans. T. W. Rhys Davids (London: Henry Frowde, 1910).

Some of you out there who've studied both mindfulness and Buddhism are now probably nodding your heads and smiling, and for those who haven't, a lot of mindfulness meditations are probably making a little more sense now.

Mindful living derives a large part of its core from Buddhism—it's as simple as that—but I've also got a little news that might just make your day. With its growing popularity, doctors have finally started taking notice of mindfulness, and people have been performing studies on what effects it might have on the brain. The results are nothing short of stellar. For instance, one study that you can read in the *International Journal of Yoga* titled "Functional Connectivity of Prefrontal Cortex in Various Meditation Techniques,"[5] published in 2022, takes twenty-three studies on meditation techniques and specifically separates the data from mindful meditation to determine what kind of activity it generates in your prefrontal cortex. That's the part of your brain that handles things like self-awareness, cognition, memory, and emotional control—just to name a few of its core functions. The study used tools like magnetic resonance imaging to see what the brain was up to during mindful meditation, as well as other types of meditation, such as transcendental, focused attention, and Sahaj yoga meditations. The results were very interesting: mindful meditation definitely lit up the prefrontal cortex, but it was also apparent that there was connected activity showing up in other parts of the brain.

So what does this mean from a practical standpoint? Well, from this particular study, we're able to see that mindfulness provides enhanced neural function with practical applications in things like:

- improved cognitive awareness

---

[5] Mrithunjay Rathore et al., "Functional Connectivity of Prefrontal Cortex in Various Meditation Techniques—A Mini-Review," *International Journal of Yoga* 15, no. 3 (2022): 187–194, https://doi.org/10.4103%2Fijoy.ijoy_88_22.

- increased alertness and focus
- better control of inhibition response
- conflict resolution awareness (as evinced in activity between the dorsolateral prefrontal cortex and the anterior cingulate cortex)
- pain management applications

These are just the tip of the iceberg—I've linked the study in the footnote above for those who want to learn more, but you get the idea. That "mindful lemonade" exercise doesn't seem like much on the surface, but like many things in life, it's got depths to it once you understand the lesson.

Living intentionally and taking a mindful approach to the world opens up a lot of doors, and when you start flexing those mindfulness muscles even more, those days of wondering "Where did all my time go?" will soon be far behind you.

You'll know exactly where they went—because you tailored and savored each and every minute that YOU decided to keep!

Chapter Two

Listen to Laughter and Smell the Roses

Time, or more accurately, our perception of time, puts on winged slippers when we let ourselves fall into too much of a routine. It's the reason why slow or exceedingly busy days in an otherwise predictable job can seem to stick out so long. So what causes time to blur out in a way that makes us wonder where the minutes went?

I'll demonstrate part of the problem with a simple joke. How many dyslexics does it change to take a lightbulb? (To be clear—I'm not making light of dyslexia but merely demonstrating a quick point about how the mind works, most of the time.) Go back and read that joke again, but hear each word individually in your mind in the order they are written. It didn't say, "How many dyslexics does it TAKE to change a lightbulb," but the majority of us read it that way the first time.

That's because the brain is geared to look for patterns, and when reliable ones pop up, your brain takes a little bit of a break and reduces "processor speed," so to speak. Your brain has a good reason to do this—if everything was new all of the time, your brain would be quite overstimulated, and that's certainly not healthy.

That said, it's still a problem—you're losing quite a lot of time this way—and mindfulness is going to give you a workable compromise to make the most of your minutes so that time will at least feel like it's being doled out more generously.

Avoiding the slippage of minutes truly is vital, especially if you are a parent. For those of you with kids out there, consider this: How many weekends do you really get to share with your kids? How many summers?

You could just count the total of actual days from infant to teen to answer this question, but it wouldn't necessarily give you the best answer. The reason for this has to do with the human brain and also developmental norms. According to Rachael Elward, PhD, an expert in the cognitive neuroscience of memory, the hippocampus of a child should be ready at about four years of age,[6] and this is good to know—this is the time that your child will start to reliably remember things.

They remember things from before this, of course, but not in the same way. Our adult memories are quite solid because of all of the associations—especially language—which allow us to invoke a host of things about a particular day that help us remember it. "Do you remember that day that Joe slipped on the ice?" For instance, a prompt like this might bring back memories of the cold and the feeling of the wind that day. Visually, you might remember that the light was dim because it was overcast, and you'll have a stored audio clip of Joe crying out in surprise.

These all tie together, but until the hippocampus is four years old, it's focusing the most processor speed on learning things like sitting up, what tastes good and what doesn't, how to get your attention, and other basics important to development. If you factor in that your kids start getting their rebellious

---

[6] Catherine Ball, "Making Memories Matters, Even If Your Baby Won't Remember Them," *Parents*, August 30, 2023, https://www.parents.com/kids/development/childhood-amnesia-heres-why-your-child-cant-remember-being-a-baby/.

streak and pushing away to become individuals at around thirteen years of age, then you're left with nine years that are considered "prime real estate" as far as childhood memories are concerned—these are the ones that are going to be easiest to recall, and knowing this helps you to take advantage of that.

In those nine years, you've got nine summers and 468 weekends...which sounds like a lot, but it isn't. Those of us who grew up in the late '70s and '80s when Saturday morning cartoons were a big deal are especially aware of that— your parents tended to rest during that time, and you were on your own. Fast-forward to now, and there are a million channels, but the same scenario tends to play out a little. So don't let this happen. Start to be mindful of that weekend time and try to do some things together. Visit the zoo or the arboretum— they're cheap and memorable. Go out camping from time to time. The kids will grumble at first, but you'll find things to do and share together, and these memories appreciate in value and mature like fine wine over time.

Of course, if you don't have children, that doesn't give you a reason to spend your weekends wastefully, either. You've only got fifty-two of them a year—so use them wisely. Keep in mind as well that most jobs start you off with only two weeks of vacation time, and many of us will spend a day here and there simply slacking—just to get a little rest! It's nice to sleep in sometimes, but if you don't start doing the math, then you're going to find that your opportunities for shared special weekends or simply solo special weekends will dwindle away. A good habit to get into is to start creating a visual representation of some of your "prime times" so that you will see them every day, and this will remind you to make the most of them.

Mindfulness Exercise: Creating a Colorful Calendar as a Visual Aid for Your "Prime Times"

One of the best ways to make sure that you are mindful of your time is to make it easy for yourself with a calendar that will show you at a glance the largest chunks of time coming up. That way, not only will you take better notice of the time that belongs EXCLUSIVELY to you, but you'll also have a head start crafting ways to make them more memorable.

Let's take a look at how it's done!

What You'll Need:

- 1 black marker
- 5 different colored highlighters—green, bright yellow, brown, light blue, black, and bright red
- 1 large calendar

How It's Done:

A mindful way to combat the blurring effects of routine is to create a visual reminder of seasonal cycles and your time off. With just a quick look, you'll be able to inventory your time and keep track of environmental factors that will be important if you want to plan realistically.

Wintertime, for instance, is a good time to stay in and read, drink hot cocoa, spend some time by a nice, roaring fire, or set up a snowball fight with the kids. Springtime is perfect for the arboretum, planting a tree, or taking a nice nature hike. Summertime is a great time to feed ducks, and if you have kids, then you can have outings later in the day after work that simply wouldn't be practical on weekdays. Fall is fantastic for getting cozy—and counting your blessings. You get the idea!

We'll mark these on the calendar with your colored highlighters. As far as colors go, you've got a green highlighter for spring, bright yellow for summer, brown for fall, and light blue for winter—but don't color these in just yet!

You're going to need to mark your days off FIRST, and bright red is a great color for this. It sticks out so that you can spot your days off easily, but it's also a very aggressive color, so mentally, you're getting a little extra "oomph" to craft something good for those bright red "me" markers. Mark out your entire two weeks of vacation time somewhere, preferably in a nice season to enjoy it. You might not intend to use it but do this anyway. You'll be surprised at the seeds that get planted when you don't simply write off your vacation time as something to do in that formless "later."

The calendar doesn't have to be fancy—you can get one at a dollar store but any department store will have plenty of calendars, and you should get a big one if you can so that you can put it somewhere you'll see it every day so that you can't ignore it.

After marking your days, you can denote seasons with a thick-line outline and diagonal lines going across the squares so that you won't be sitting there all day coloring them. You might think this seems simplistic, but try it for a month, and you'll see for yourself that it has some appreciable hidden depths.

By placing your mindful calendar somewhere you'll see it first thing every morning, you're putting thoughts in motion for mindful planning that goes into play well before you're even fully awake. This helps to ensure that you don't overlook the possibilities. You'll always know at a glance how much free time you have and the color-coding will help you to comprehend it instantly.

Put your black marker somewhere nearby (Velcro tape is an easy way to pull this off so that it doesn't get misplaced—you can stick it close on the wall If you like) and mark each day as it passes. Just like that "watched pot" never seems to boil, so does "watched time" become much less likely to be something that you'll waste.

Now that you've created a visual representation of the best times to work with, how do you stretch your minutes a little further? By choosing the types of moments that you want to have and by exploiting "sensory loopholes," of course!

Mindfulness Exercise: Making a Morning Meditation Box

Meditation in the morning is a great way to help ensure that you're going to have a mindful approach for the day ahead of you. In this exercise, I'll tell you how to make a morning meditation box that you can use for meditation and as a way to get your subconscious and conscious mind on the same page before starting your day.

What You'll Need:

- 1 small box—it can be a mini trunk, a shoebox, etc. The important part is that you can use it to stow away a few items for daily meditation use.

- 1 spare plastic box or bin to store extra items and ones you've already used so that you can shuffle them back into the mix.

- assorted items that can be used to help stimulate sight, hearing, touch, smell, and taste (see the instructions below).

Making the Box:

Making the box itself is actually quite a lot of fun. Set yourself a small budget so that you won't be tempted to go overboard and acquire at least two items for each sense listed below to get started. The examples below are just to give you an idea of what we're aiming for together—anything that fits which you prefer is fine. That said, here are those examples:

- **Sight:** An easy way to get a sight prop is to simply get a small coffee table art book that will fit in the box you've chosen. Preferably one with different artists so that everything is new, but if you prefer to get contemplative with a favorite artist every morning, then hey—it's your box, and that's fine. Other options are anything with detail to look at, really. For instance, interesting coins, seashells, or whatever else seems to please your eyes.

- **Smell:** Essential oils are a good option, and you can take the labels off them so that you can uncap the container and let the scents fill the air. Scratch and sniff stickers are still out there if you want to order some on Amazon and things like flower petals and dried fruits also have a distinctive smell of their own.

- **Hearing:** Pieces of metal to clink together, bells, little drums, and Druid balls (silver balls with springs inside that make a sound like what you hear when a wizard in a TV show casts a spell). You can also play music on shuffle and use a surprise song for this part of your meditation; I find that this variation can sometimes spice up a morning meditation perfectly.

- **Touch:** Small swathes of fabric work well for this, like cotton, velvet, and silk, but you can also use things with a natural texture like seashells, stones, crystals (cool and angular, which is always interesting)—anything that moves the needle from a tactile perspective.

- **Taste:** While there are a lot of ways you can meet this requirement—including packaged candies, dried fruits, and such—one fun way to store the taste components of your meditations is one of those plastic Monday-through-Sunday pill boxes. The tiny compartments are perfect for little food, spice, drink mix packets, or candy samples, and if you add your items quickly and stow them away, then you'll forget what's in there until you get a taste of it.

Pick two of each of these items for your box and try to surprise yourself a little—if they can go into a little pouch to stay hidden until you pull them out, that's a lot better, but don't stress yourself too much on it. Your focus is going to sharpen either way if you stick to the meditation, and after you make your first meditation box, you'll inevitably create improvements of your own.

How to Use Your Morning Meditation Box:

1. Set aside about thirty minutes each morning for this mediation and it should be just about perfect. Keep in mind that the order for each is not set in stone—I like doing the "hearing" portion last so that I'm starting the day off with sharpened senses and musical reinforcement at the end.

2. Find somewhere comfortable to sit and set a timer for thirty minutes. A kitchen timer is perfect, but DO NOT use your phone. Getting a phone call or a text when you're deeply in contemplation is a jarring experience and one best avoided. After sitting down and setting that time, begin your breathing exercise—a simple three-three-three (inhale for a count of three, hold for a count of three, and exhale for a count of three) until you are breathing that way without counting.

3. Spend five minutes doing the exercise for each of the senses. For example purposes, we'll use the order listed previously, so we're starting with sight. Pick up your sight prop and put all of your focus into contemplating it. Is it colorful? What colors are used

together? Are they complimentary or clashing? What patterns do you see, and can you break them down to basic circle and triangle shapes in your mind? Let your mind wander a little and explore the image in your way—the questions I listed are just to give you an idea of how to start.

4. Moving on to smell, pull out one of your vials with a label removed and uncap it at chest level. If you've picked something else, like a piece of Sulfur or some dried fruit, then simply sniff it carefully and do it again with your eyes closed. Think about what it reminds you of—is this scent tied to any memories? What do you like and dislike about it? Again, just see where your mind goes, and after five minutes of contemplation, we'll move on to hearing.

5. If you've gone with the MP3 player, you can queue up a random song, and it's OK if it doesn't hit the full five minutes—just close your eyes and let the music soak in. See if you can pick out different instruments individually, and contrast their sound to the singer if the music is not strictly instrumental. If you're going with a prop, tap the drum or ring the bell and see where it takes your mind and then when you're ready, we can move on to touch.

6. Pull an item out of the bag if you hid these or directly from the box if you didn't, and close your eyes and focus on the tactile sensation of handling it. Is it smooth or coarse? Can you build an image of the item in your mind based on just what you are feeling? Put all your focus into it and explore the item thoroughly—we're now ready for the final sense in this example—taste.

7. Pop the top on the box for the day that you're doing the meditation, or get your sample from the container that you decided to use and give it a taste. Consider it first with your eyes

open, and then close them and do it again. Do you notice more with your eyes closed? What seems to change about the flavor? Does it taste natural or chemical? Sweet or sour? Get to know the flavor well enough, and later down the line, you can even prepare mixes to see if you can pick them out!

This is a meditation that you can do as often as you like—be it daily, twice a week, or simply once a week, but it's a great way to help teach yourself to enjoy your five senses to the fullest. After you've got two of each item to get started, just keep an eye out for things that you can add to the second box so that you can switch items regularly and keep the meditation fresh!

In time you'll notice that you're paying attention to the world around you in a very different way, and it's really quite the revelation—this minute matters, indeed!

Picking Your Perfect Moments and Exploiting Sensory Loopholes

When you start getting good at focusing on the minutiae that really matters, then this is going to help you pick and choose more worthwhile ways to savor your time, as well as increase the intensity with which you may experience these things.

Putting your focus toward absorbing a particular sight, sound, scent, feel, or taste creates a sensory loophole for your time that's really quite amazing, and it makes perfect sense when you think about it. After all, your mind is used to your daily routine, and as I've mentioned, it will devote less "processor time" to the same stimuli that it comes to expect. When you experience one of those things in a mindful way, you're giving your brain some interesting new data to work with, and the performance jump can feel almost surreal.

For those of you with kids, think of the first time that you've ever heard your child laughing. It's a pure sound, untouched by the years, and really quite contagious—it's almost impossible not to smile! A simple joy like that is one that you can enjoy year after year. The things that amuse your child change, and by taking the time to appreciate it, you'll also become closer by learning what they like.

I'll take a moment to share two mindfulness exercises for the parents out there but don't worry—there's another one after that for those who would prefer something they can do on their own or simply share with someone special!

Mindfulness Exercise: Laugh Tracks

There is nothing quite like the laugh of a child, or even better, laughs that you've shared. This little exercise can help you to be mindful of every time that you hear one, and if you stick to it for a few years, you're going to have a keepsake that you wouldn't sell for all of the money in the world. Intrigued? Keep reading, and you'll see what I mean!

What You'll Need:

- 1 portable handheld recorder (see notes)
- a thirty-minute to one-hour time commitment every week (don't worry—it's time well spent!)

One of the saddest pitfalls in life that we only truly learn in later years is that we're so convinced that we'll NEVER forget something that we don't even try to save a piece of it. Don't believe me? Well, think of the most exotic vacation that you've ever gone on. Do you remember every second?

Of course not! While some memories are locked in there that might pop out at random times due to an associated smell or some imagery on a show that you're watching, without a reliable trigger you can't call a specific memory instantly 100 percent of the time.

Invest in a portable recording device for this exercise. They're pretty easy to find in the electronics section of any department store and designed so that creative types can leave memos to themselves and importantly, you want the type that will save to a file format that you can put on your computer.

If you're on a tight budget, your phone can already do this, but I really recommend getting a device that you'll only use for this exercise. The sound quality is generally better, for one thing, and for another, you won't have to worry that someone sending you a message or calling you on the phone interrupts the preservation of a truly fantastic laugh.

Of course, this brings us to the next part—how do you get someone to laugh honestly? Well, kids are pretty easy in this regard. You can hide your recorder in your pocket or nearby if you are at home and try one of the following:

- watch your kid's favorite cartoon with them
- read a favorite funny book together
- leave your recorder running during a birthday party

You can expand on these ideas in little ways—get creative—for instance, you can go together to the bookstore every week or two and have a contest to find the funniest book. Just don't stress if you miss a laugh or two—you'll miss bunches—but the ones that you get can be filed away on your computer with a date and backed up in another one or two spots, and then they are yours forever.

Imagine later down the line, when your child is about to go to college, sharing a photo slideshow of happy moments over the years and real sound bites of family laughter—like the old sitcom "laugh tracks," but so much better. As far as keepsakes go, it doesn't get more precious than THAT!

Mindfulness Exercise: Pieces of Childhood

Kids love to draw, and while the fridge is probably already covered with their art, it might surprise you how many ways you can stretch these little blessings to get a little more "mindful mileage" out of them. Below you'll find an example that I think you'll like—Making a puzzle that you can do together and save as a keepsake!

What You'll Need:

- 1 blank puzzle (available through local and online craft shops)
- small boxes
- clear box frames

Did you know that you can buy blank puzzles? Arts and craft stores are treasure troves for an almost unlimited number of mindfulness exercises, and blank puzzles are really quite popular. You can purchase ones that are very easy to solve for young children, let them draw on them in permanent colored marker, and then stick the pieces in a box to solve together and store for later.

If your kid gets bored with the easy ones, don't worry—arts and crafts stores, both local and online, have blank puzzles at varying levels of difficulty, and you can get creative with the drawings on them. For instance, you can both make pictures for the other to color in!

The clear box frames give you a way to display the Best Puzzle of the Week or whatever category you choose to highlight, and unbeknownst to the kids, mom and dad can always save a favorite and preserve it later with acrylic or glue to sock away in the old keepsakes chest.

Shared moments like this are a great way to be mindful of shared time with your family. While your kids will draw every day for an artistic phase that may or may not persist through their lifetimes, you can milk these moments for all that they're worth by simply choosing the mediums.

That way, you won't discourage your kids by making too many rules—you've just traded cardboard for drawing paper—and you've created some new possibilities of what you can do with the resulting, priceless art and a deviation from the norm that will help to cement these moments in everyone's memories!

Mindfulness Exercise: Fairy Flowers

I promised an exercise that may be done solo, as well as shared, and so this takes us to fairy flowers (or fairest flowers, if you prefer).

You've probably heard that "you need to take time to smell the flowers," and while it's a trite phrase, it's always been a true one. A good way to make sure that you take the time out to do this is to make something fun out of it that you can do with the kids or someone else who is special in your life.

It starts with an arboretum ticket, and you'll find the rest of the instructions below!

What You'll Need:

- cheap notepads (one for each of you)

- pencils (or pens)
- arboretum tickets

Depending on whether this is solo or shared, the premise goal is pretty malleable. With kids, you could tell them that the goal is to find the fairest flower in the arboretum, where a fairy might be most likely to make their home. If that's got a little too much "flight of fancy" for you, or if you are doing this exercise with a partner, then it's simply a hunt for the fairest flower in the arboretum—as a way to sharpen up your mindful thinking.

The notepads will be for grading the flowers—based on color, shapes, and scents—but feel free to make your own scoring system. Maybe a flower will lose points for thorns or even gain them as a "defense" against the flower being plucked and interrupting the "fairy" while they're having tea.

Have fun with it—smelling the flowers is one of those pleasures we're quick to lose as children, and it's a fine one to take back into your life!

At the end of the day, you can take photos with the flower or you could make a quick timed contest out of this exercise as a way to decide where to have a picnic.

Mind you...You can certainly "stop and smell the flowers" at any time—and you SHOULD—but by injecting your will into it and making the moment more memorable, you'll be taking much better control of your time.

As an added bonus, when you're doing this exercise with someone else, you'll also be planting the seeds of a nostalgic habit that can lead to more mindful lives of their own—think of it as "stop and smell the flowers" with a little upgrade!

Evolving Your Process—Switching Things up to Keep Your Moments More Memorable

Now that you're getting a little better at attenuating your senses to properly savor the moment and at picking things you'd like to do, you're going to notice something—your goals are going to change a little over time.

Not only that, but it gets easier to accomplish them. Like a book, life is all about the journey, and when you start experiencing your own life again instead of trying to rush to the last page, you'll be surprised by what you can enjoy that seemed blasé before.

In order to keep exploiting the loophole, you'll want to always experiment with mindful appreciation of what's around you in different ways. It's a lot easier than you think! Bubble baths with Fizzmos—fizzy balls that release the scent and soften the water—can relax you and delight the senses.

For those who like DIY, slowing down to focus not only on the work, but the scents of the cut wood, the metals and oils, and some extra attention to detail work can make a project into something more like a meditation!

To help ensure that you keep setting goals and thus evolving the process, and also to help you learn to take advantage of those extra stimuli to exercise enhanced recall, I'm including two journal exercises here and you can use one, the other, or combine the two if you like.

First, I'll explain the benefits of each, and then we'll move on to the next chapter, where we can rediscover a classic mindfulness extravaganza—the kind you create in your kitchen!

Mindfulness Exercise: Goals and Gratefulness Journal

While there are a lot of things you can do with a journal, I think one of the most overlooked and most useful ones is making a goals and gratefulness journal. The reason that it's important is that the moment things go south, we tend to forget the little things that we really appreciate, and let's face it—goals are more often mentioned than pursued. That's because these are things that you NEED to be actively mindful of and I'll tell you the easiest way to do it.

What You'll Need:

- 1 blank journal
- 1 pen

History tells us that one of the last great Roman emperors, Marcus Aurelius, had a little mindfulness journal of his own. Every morning he would wake up and write down what he had accomplished from the day before, what he intended to do that day, and even who he thought that he might meet and disagree with—so that he could try to "forgive them in advance" and thus take control of potential stress that might otherwise sour his day.

That's all good and well if you're an emperor, but we've got really busy schedules, so why not take a few minutes with your first coffee to do something a little faster and arguably just as useful?

Get in the habit of bringing your journal with you to the table for your first morning coffee, or if you like, simply keep it at your bedside and scribble a few things underneath the date before you get out of bed. Jot down five things that you are grateful for first and then one thing that you'd like to accomplish that day or this week. Don't stress yourself with it—simply pick something realistic so that you don't get frustrated. This will help you to be more mindful by focusing on the things that make life worthwhile and also by stating your will somewhere outside of your thoughts. The next day, if you accomplished that goal, then mention it and underline it after you've scribbled in the five things you are grateful for. If you didn't accomplish it, that's OK; just write down that you want to do it so that it's kept active in your mind.

It's strange, but writing something down keeps things fresh in your mind where you can make the most use of them. By taking a quick inventory of some things you are grateful for and a single goal that you want to achieve, you'll start each day with a better attitude and a more productive one. Try it for a week, and you'll see for yourself—you'll get more done, and if you ever need a reminder about what really matters in life, you can just flip through the pages you've written in and see those things chronicled in your neat (or not so neat) handwriting.

Mindfulness Exercise: Journaling for Non-Journalers— Creating a Quip Journal

Journaling is not for everyone. For some of us, it's just too darned personal, and the thought of someone coming across a journal and peeking into our private thoughts makes these useful books into something that's simply too taboo.

There's a way around that problem that I detail below which I hope you will try. You'll be very happy that you did, and I tell you how in the instructions below.

What You'll Need:

- 1 blank journal (small and portable)
- 1 pen

One thing that I've learned while traveling is that pictures of the places you've visited don't have the same kind of impact on your memory that you might expect. Without going into too much detail, I can give you the gist of it—I'd taken some photos of various bits of nature in a few different parts of Europe, thinking, "This is so beautiful I don't need to label these right away, I'll NEVER forget them." A few months down the line, I was sorting photos, and I found out the hard way that you can forget just about anything if you don't take a mindful approach. Luckily for me, I was experimenting with a quip journal, and as it turned out, IT WORKED.

To make a quip journal, all you need is a blank journal (preferably one you can clip a pen inside) that is small enough that you can easily carry it with you to scribble in whenever you like. The cool part of a quip journal is this: you don't have to write paragraphs; just jot down a sentence every now and again that describes something you saw that day.

Examples:

- Grumpy old man keeps smiling; his grandchild's fault.

- Vivid sights, but the fish market is "louder."

- Toe hurts; not tellin' the kids.

Here's the secret—keep your sentences short and sweet and be vague about the context. Some hardcore journalers will tell you that you have to capture every little detail in your journal, but that's simply not true. All I had for those photos that I suddenly found I couldn't categorize was their dates were a few seemingly random sentences I jotted down without giving much thought to. And a funny thing happened when I read them: my mind took me to the EXACT place I'd written them in. I didn't get an automated voice in my head saying something like "Bucharest, 12 o'clock, coordinates 44.4268° N, 26.1025° E"—it was much more meaningful and amazing than that.

That single sentence gave me a much more mindful experience—the sights and scents of the day, the memory of driving, and walking to that place. Lunch and snacks that I enjoyed that day. It all came flooding back, prompted by a handful of seemingly nonsensical sentences.

Try it sometime, and you'll see for yourself if you don't believe me. If you are deadset against journaling, then prove me wrong. Get a small journal and scribble one sentence—however nonsensical it seems—that describes one weird thing you saw that day. Do this for a week, then look at it a month later and see where your mind goes.

If it works for you, then get in the habit of scribbling random sentences in a journal, and what you'll have now is something very precious indeed—a time machine that can bring mindful moments into the present any time that you like and best of all, no one else can translate the darned thing. Those sentences are mindful markers that only you can decipher! Pretty cool, no? Personally, I'm really glad now that I never labeled those photos—it just reinforced for me that taking an active role and doing little mindful experiments always pays off—and I got to keep those precious moments I thought I'd accidentally lost.

With that said, let's move on together to rediscover the amazing wonders of cooking with love for building nostalgia and making every minute count!

Chapter Three

Cook with Love

Cooking is one of the most rewarding mindful exercises that you can do and the proof in the pudding is probably already there in your memories. If you had a parent or grandparent who liked to cook for you, it's a special feeling that comes with a flood of memories of scent, taste, texture, and even the sounds of the kitchen.

Whether you are alone or preparing a meal for yourself and someone special, nothing says this minute matters like a little cooking with love! In this chapter, we'll cover the subject just enough to get you a solid starting point for a little culinary exploration of your own.

Oh, and did I mention we'll be cooking things up from scratch? Don't worry—all of the recipes in this chapter are simple, and we're just going to go over some basic flavor profiles and make a few quick substitutions that can really pack a punch.

A Mindful Practice That Pays Delectable Dividends at the End!

As a mindfulness exercise, cooking with love is definitely one of the best ways to go. You get to enjoy fantastic tastes, sampling ingredients and checking to see if your food is seasoned. Then you've got the fantastic smells wafting through the kitchen.

Sizzling, bubbling, and mixing all have their own rhythms, and the heat intensity that you use helps you craft and shape your dishes to the textures and richness you like. When it's done, a little garnish on the side makes for a lovely presentation, and then you're ready to savor each bit on your own or with a little conversation if you're sharing with someone special.

In our nine-to-five rat race, we've gotten so used to instant gratification in the food department that it's easy to forget how special a homemade meal really is. The thing is, while it's not been heavily studied, there is some research out there that attributes a lot of our modern stress to our increased reliance on instant meals and further, that cooking has a lot of personal benefits for the one whipping up those fantastic meals.

Why Cooking from Scratch Is the Way to Go—The Benefits of Taking Your Time

So that you know I'm not pulling your leg about studies, one example with a really verbose title is called "Well-Being and Cooking Behavior: Using the Positive Emotion, Engagement, Relationships, Meaning, and Accomplishment (PERMA) Model as a Theoretical Framework," and it was published by the *Frontiers in Psychology* journal.[7] This study covered a lot of aspects of cooking from both a practical and a psychological standpoint, and the results are really pretty interesting. For instance, to cook well, the skills you have to develop fall into the categories of planning, cognitive, perceptual, and mechanical. Simply put, it takes a lot of mindful

---

[7] Nicole Farmer, and Elizabeth W. Cotter, "Well-Being and Cooking Behavior: Using the Positive Emotion, Engagement, Relationships, Meaning, and Accomplishment (PERMA) Model as a Theoretical Framework," *Frontiers in Psychology* 12 (April 2021): 560578, https://doi.org/10.3389/fpsyg.2021.560578.

thinking to transform an assortment of seemingly unrelated ingredients into a yummy, cohesive meal. Use of these skills can trigger neurobiological activation in your brain, which comes with a very positive wellness boost that may explain why Gramma or Dad was always so sweet after cooking up a meal for you from scratch!

A second benefit that the study found is that cooking skills are heavily reflected in the skills that you need throughout your life—such as problem-solving and planning.

One final thing that should be noted: the reason I recommend taking your time and learning to cook things from scratch was actually something mentioned in the study. Cooking with most of your food already prepared was found to actually be a source of stress much of the time—it usually boiled down to a missing ingredient or two that became a frustrating barrier to the expected lunch or dinner.

By learning substitutions, as well as basic food profiles like FASHion cooking (more on this shortly), you can make everything from scratch and reap all of the mindful and practical benefits that come with kitchen art.

It's One of the Most Wonderful Ways to Show a Loved One That This Minute Matters

The time when cooking with love really makes this minute matter is with your loved ones. Even if Mom or Dad weren't good at cooking, you probably miss their boxed mac and cheese, and no matter how you try, yours never tastes the same. It's a little like that, although if you get that someone special to help you cook it can be even more!

Sometimes Your Cooking Can Also Say the Things You Can't

Spoken communication doesn't come easily to everyone, and for some folks, words seem like a shallow outlet for such strong emotion when you can express your love in your actions instead. Cooking is an excellent way to display your affection—it's unmistakably personal, and your careful planning, attention to detail, and knowledge of your special someone's favorites can really go a long way toward bringing you closer.

Moreover, you're going to get a lot of the same psychological benefits as if you'd had that meaningful chat instead and the natural endorphin boost from a healthy, home-cooked will support you well into the rest of the day and strengthen you for any challenges you're expecting to come.

Now that I've covered some of the practical and psychological benefits, it's time for the fun part—learning a little about cooking from scratch! While this is by no means a comprehensive guide, what I CAN give you is just enough to get you started and hopefully a little intrigued.

In the crash course, I cover FASHion cooking (don't worry, it's just a little acronym I'll introduce to help you remember the four basic foundation ingredients you need), substitutions for when you're out of ingredients or want to shake things up a bit, and a few basic recipes you can tweak. If you're ready, then let's get this kitchen party started!

Cooking from Scratch—A Quick Crash Course to Get You Started

There's only so much you can teach in one section of a lone chapter, but I wanted to pack in some basics and a framework of tips that can help you to get started and avoid some common pitfalls to avoid getting frustrated.

Use your mindful thinking tactics as you go—get to know the textures, scents, sights, cooking sounds, and tastes of foods in various stages of the cooking process and focus on what you are doing. It's a mindful meditation like no other, and if you put in the effort, you and your loved ones can reap the benefits for a lifetime.

I start off by giving you some basic tips to keep in mind when you are experimenting with from-scratch recipes, and after that, I touch on a FASHion flavor profile foundation (fat, acid, salt, heat—it's on NOW!) and the importance of learning substitute ingredients.

Hungry yet? Let's get started!

Useful Tips for Scratch-Cooking for Beginners

While you are teaching yourself some basic cooking from scratch, here are a few tips to keep in mind:

- Find your favorite salt. Experiment with different salts beyond your regular old table salt—sea salt, pink salt, flavored salts—and play with textures and different cuts as well. Flaked salt, for instance, definitely has a charm, and you can rediscover this essential spice by simply twisting the texture range for your palette.

- Apply bouncing rules for your pan. Hard stuff goes into the pan first. For instance, if you're chopping onions, you'll get harder and softer bits, so add the hard ones first to let them cook more to soften. This applies to all of your ingredients. Play with the high and low settings as well when you do this, and watch what happens. You can still make crispy bacon or grilled onions with a slow cook and a lower setting, and the results are often exquisite.

- Try to resist mixing in advance. Unless a recipe calls for it, try to avoid mixing things in advance. Mindful cooking takes longer, but it's worth it, and you'll develop an intuitive sense for cooking that comes with experience—you'll know how foods should look slow-cooked or seared, how they smell when flavors are blending, and more. You will never get that if you rush through this, so take your time EVERY time.

- Always taste before seasoning. You can always add spice, but balancing out your dish when you overdo it can really spoil your day. Taste first, add a little spice, and taste again. It's not a race, and I can guarantee you that along the way, you're going to learn the perfect amounts of your favorite spices with each individual dish (and it's SO much better than "shake and pray").

- A cold pan is asking for trouble. You always want to preheat your pan, as a cold pan can lead to an uneven cook, but a preheated pan already in the optimal heat range for your dish is something you can really work magic with.

- Keep it simple. Stick to simple recipes in the beginning unless you're just having so much fun that you want to hazard something more complicated. A lot of simple recipes are FANTASTIC—think of the flavor profile of the classic peanut butter and jelly sandwich. A recipe doesn't have to be rocket science to work.

- Be patient and have fun. If you stick with simple scratch recipes and allow yourself to have fun with them, you're going to learn and get really good at whipping up wonderful things in your kitchen. If you burn something or don't cook something enough, fix it if you can or scrap it, but don't get discouraged. Take the mindful approach and then every failure is just a lesson that will make you even better.

Remember FASHion—Fat, Acid, Salt, Heat—It's on NOW!

A great way to help make sure that your experiments in culinary mindfulness don't go too far off the rails is to remember the FASHion acronym—fat, acid, salt, and heat.

Every basic meal should have a mix of these things, and if it does, you'll be amazed by what this simple formula can do. Don't believe me? If you have a Netflix account, you can look for a show called *Fat Acid Salt Heat* and see Chef Samin Nosrat traveling the world and trying out different recipes that reflect this culinary standard. You can also get a copy of her book[8] if you would like to learn more, but I explain the basics and how to put them to good use in the following sections.

FASHion—The interplay of the four basics:

- **Fat** adds texture and flavor.

- **Acid** balances out flavors so they aren't overwhelming.

- **Salt** is another flavor building block.

- **Heat** helps everything come together and determines the finished texture.

Sources for FASHion basics

- **Fat:** Vegetable oil, butter, lard, or even fruit and nut oils—you've got plenty of options for flavorful fat that can turn a simple recipe into something superb.

---

[8] Samin Nosrat, *Salt, Fat, Acid, Heat: Mastering the Elements of Good Cooking* (New York: Simon and Schuster, 2017).

- **Acid:** Wines, vinegar, and things like yogurt, sour cream, and buttermilk are all good examples of acid, but there are a few you might not think of like cocoa and molasses. Expand your knowledge of these ingredients, and you won't believe some of the odd combos that really WORK.

- **Salt:** Table salt, pink salt, sea salt—different kinds pack different punches, and experimenting with them will definitely open some flavor doors. You can also achieve the salt factor with other ingredients, such as soy sauce, miso, or anchovies—just to give you a few ideas.

- **Heat:** Don't think of heat as merely temperature—but rather texture. A preheated pan that is oiled and hot enough can sear a crunch on the outside, while leaving your food soft inside, or help you fry a perfect egg that is crispy on the bottom and has a yummy runny yolk.

Substitutions—Learn Them and Play with Them

One of the little life lessons you can learn from cooking is the beauty of substitutions—if you can't get exactly what you want, sometimes there's a comparable scenario that you might find you like even better.

One good example of this is when you are making a cake, you can substitute one of the eggs with a 1/4 cup of unsweetened applesauce. Your cake will still taste fantastic, but guess what? It will also make your cake extra moist! You can also use a 1/4 cup of buttermilk, yogurt, or mashed banana to the same effect, and each adds its own unique touch to your creation.

Do you want buttermilk flavor but you're fresh out of buttermilk? You can add a tablespoon of vinegar (white or apple cider) or lemon juice to your cup then fill it up to the one cup mark with regular milk. Stir it and let it thicken for a few minutes and it's ready to go!

Small recipe substitutions are good to learn and if you combine them with simple recipes, then you're going to find that you have a new superpower—being able to whip something simple and yummy up from scratch from whatever is in the pantry! You can also interchange other aspects of recipes, with cheese being a great example that can produce some serious taste differences to jazz up an old favorite. Here are some quick examples to give you an idea:

- Colby and sharp cheddar can each stand in for the other as needed.

- Mild cheddar, Monterey Jack, mozzarella, and sometimes provolone may be interchanged in a recipe.

- Tired of parmesan? Switch things up with pecorino.

We won't go into a lot of detail on these, but you get the idea—try one or more of the examples from this section and see what happens. With a little substitution practice and just a handful of simple recipes, you'll have so many variations of your favorite meals to play with that you'll be very happy you invested the time!

Simple Recipes You Can Make from Scratch

Well, here we are, the recipes! Below you will find six simple recipes that you can make on your own from scratch. Each one is useful in its own way, as the recipe can be tweaked and adapted with substitutions so that you can create many delicious variations on the classic foundation you'll be starting with.

The included recipes below are:

- whole wheat pancakes
- creamy potato and leek soup
- mushroom and chicken risotto (or it can be simply mushroom risotto if you don't eat meat)
- homemade skillet pizza
- chunky homemade applesauce
- delicious DIY ranch dressing (Oh yes, this one is a HIT at home!)

Hungry yet? I know that I am, so let's get started with some recipes that will get you cooking with love in no time flat!

Whole Wheat Pancakes—A Timeless Classic They'll Always Crave

One of the easiest recipes that gets the most mileage is pancakes, and whole wheat pancakes take that classic flavor to a new level. For one thing, despite being healthier for you, they're actually more flavorful than your average box mix white flour pancakes, and they also stay moist if you want to fold one up with a little honey in a Ziploc bag for snacking later!

Try making them yourself, and for giggles, try substituting a 1/4 cup of unsweetened applesauce for the egg sometimes when you've made them a few times using the recipe below. It's an easy way to see how cooking from scratch tricks like substitution can make one simple recipe like this into dozens of "pancakey" possibilities!

This recipe takes twenty-five minutes total between prep and cook time and will fill up three lucky loved ones.

Ingredients:

- 1 cup buttermilk
- 1 cup whole wheat flour
- 1 egg
- 2 tbsp melted butter
- 2 tsp sugar
- 1/2 tsp baking powder
- 1/4 tsp baking soda
- 1/4 tsp salt
- butter slices (to grease your griddle)

Steps to Make:

1. Get a nice, big bowl and add in your wheat flour, sugar, salt, baking soda, and baking powder. Mix them up well together and then grab another large bowl from the cupboard.

2. In the second bowl, mix up your buttermilk, eggs, and melted butter with a wire whisk (or a spoon and sheer willpower).

3. Start pouring and whisking your wet bowl ingredients into the dry bowl, mixing well but—and this is IMPORTANT—leaving the lumps. That baking soda in your mix is reacting to the liquid, so just combine them well enough that loose flour gets wet but don't whip the mix completely smooth or your pancakes won't be light and fluffy.

4. Preheat a nonstick griddle or a large frying pan to 375 degrees. A laser thermometer can give you an exact reading and is worth the investment, but depending on your stovetop, this could be medium-high or high. Don't worry too much—you'll learn the perfect settings for your stove. Just have fun with it, and you'll pick this up FAST.

5. Using a tablespoon or a cookie scoop, add 2–3 scoops of batter to see how big of a pancake it will make—the first pancake is kind of "sacrificial," as it helps you to gauge how much batter to use and also if the pan has heated up enough to cook them properly.

6. Let your pancake cook, focusing your attention on the middle. Look for bubbling—this will let you know when it's time to flip the pancake, but you can also lift it a little with the spatula to get an idea of how much they are browning. When you see those bubbles, note the volume for future reference and flip your pancake.

7. Let your pancake cook for a bit and check the bottom by peeking a little with your spatula—in time you'll learn EXACTLY how long the perfect pancakes take, based on your own stove and the experience you're building now.

8. Repeat the process to make more pancakes, stacking them on a plate (put a little unmelted butter on top of each if you like for the pancake over it to melt), and you can put another plate on top if you like.

9. Serve your pancakes any way you like—with fruit, topped with maple syrup, or maybe a little maple mixed with molasses—get creative and find out your and your family's favorites. Congratulations—you've just made one of America's favorite staple breakfast foods from scratch!

Creamy Potato and Leek Soup—A Creamy Soup You Can Customize

Learning a basic cream soup will give you a foundation that you can definitely play with. The majority of these types of soups are built basically the same and you can make substitutions (veggie broth instead of chicken broth, for instance).

The key to perfecting your creation is at the finish, when you add your salt and acids, so be sure to take your time building this soup from scratch and then play with the recipe later.

You'll be very happy that you did!

This recipe takes about one hour and twenty minutes and will yield eight bowls of yummy and creamy potato leek soup.

Ingredients:

- 8 cups leeks (about 4 large leeks) large leeks (about 8 cups), just use white and green parts, cut into 1/2-inch thick crescents

- 7 cups water

- 6 large Yukon Gold potatoes (peeled and quartered into 1/2 inch thickness)

- 2 cups celery (4 stalks, chopped—save the leaves for garnish)

- 1 cup whole milk

- 2 tbsp and 1 tsp chicken stock base (homemade eventually; for now, store-bought is OK)

- 2 tbsp unsalted butter

- 1 tbsp olive oil

- 1 1/2 tsp kosher salt

- 1/2 teaspoon black pepper

- 1/4 cup heavy cream

- 1 dash of nutmeg (grate it fresh—it's wonderful!)

- crushed potato chips and a handful of fresh chives for garnish

Steps to Make:

1. Start things off with the sensory delight of melting your butter with your olive oil at a medium heat in a large-capacity, thick-bottomed saucepan. Add in your leeks, stirring them and enjoying the sharp scents, and let them cook in the butter and oil until softened—usually between 5 to 7 minutes.

2. Toss in your celery and do the same, stirring frequently and keeping an eye on the color. They should soften up to the perfect tenderness in about 7 to 8 minutes, and then it's time to add your potatoes.

3. Putting your potatoes into the saucepan, give them a good stir so that the sweet-scented, buttery oil gives your potatoes a shiny new coat.

4. Reduce your heat to low, and stir often, and your potatoes should get a silken, somewhat milky shine to them as the starches solidify. This should take about 5 to 6 minutes.

5. At this time, go ahead and add your chicken (or vegetable) stock and switch your heat to high, until you get a nice, bubbly boil in your pot.

6. Reduce the heat to medium and let your soup simmer for about 15 minutes—the potatoes and other veggies should be nice and softened by now—and remove the saucepan from the heat.

7. Using a ladle or a clean measuring cup, remove 2 cups of liquid from your soup, and put them in a large bowl to set to the side for now. Let your soup sit for about 30 minutes, and we are ready for the next step.

8. It's time to add stir in your cream, milk, nutmeg, salt, and pepper. You can add in some of the soup that we set aside if you want to customize the consistency, just be sure to stir it in a little at a time until you're happy with it.

9. At this point, you can serve it up in 8 bowls as is, or if you want it completely creamy, you can put it in your blender with the extra liquid we set aside and blend for about 15–20 seconds per batch. Be sure to add your final garnish before serving—chives, celery leaves, and crushed-up potato chips—and enjoy your soup!

10. If 8 bowls are too many, then don't sweat it—you can freeze it for up to 3 months in single-serving size containers if you puree it first (otherwise, the potatoes can taste a little grainy when you defrost), and you'll have a quick and easy homemade treat to enjoy later!

Mushroom and Chicken Risotto—How to Whip Up Rice Italian-style

Risotto is one of those dishes that sounds hard but is really quite easy to make—you've just got to pay attention. It's similar to making rice the way you already do at home, except that instead of boiling it up in plain ol' water, you're going to have broth and white wine soaking into that rice for a serious flavor upgrade.

If you're vegetarian, you can always double-up the mushrooms and leave the chicken out, and it will still come out fantastic, so if you're ready to learn how to make risotto from scratch, then let's get this Italian home-cooking party started!

This recipe will take just under an hour to make and yields 4 servings.

Ingredients:

- 2/3 lb boneless, skinless chicken breasts (sliced into 1/2-inch thick chunks)
- 1/2 lb mushrooms (sliced thin)
- 5 1/2 cups homemade chicken stock (or low-sodium canned chicken broth is OK for now)
- 1 1/2 cups arborio rice
- 1/2 cup onion (chopped)
- 1/2 cup of your favorite dry white wine
- 1/2 cup grated Parmesan cheese (and a little extra to add to taste)
- 2 tbsp fresh parsley (chopped)
- 2 tbsp butter
- 1 tbsp vegetable oil
- 1 tsp kosher salt (divided into 1/4 and 3/4 tsp sizes)
- 1/4 tsp black pepper (freshly ground)

Steps to Make:

1. Start things off by grabbing a large pot and adding your butter, which we're going to start melting on medium heat. Add in your mushrooms, and for the next 5 minutes, stir them occasionally as they brown and file this delicious scent away in your memory banks.

2. Now that your mushrooms are good and browned, it's time to add your chicken, along with 1/4 tsp of kosher salt and 1/4 tsp of pepper. Let your chicken cook for a good 3 to 4 minutes, and then move the contents of the pot to a separate container for now.

3. Leave the pot on the stove, but add a companion in the form of a medium saucepan on the burner next to it. Add your broth and bring it to a simmer, and we're ready for the next step.

4. Add your oil to the big pot and heat it on the low setting for a minute or 2, and then add in your onions. Let them cook, stirring occasionally, until they're almost see-through.

5. Add your rice, and stir it in the oil for about 2 minutes or until it becomes opaque. At this point, you can stir in your white wine and add that remaining 3/4 tsp of kosher salt.

6. When you can see that the wine has been absorbed into your rice, then add approximately 1/2 cup of your broth on the burner "next door" and stir this into your rice until it is absorbed as well. Make sure that the rice looks like it's simmering—it should have visible bubbling when it's at the perfect temperature, so adjust it a little if you need to before the next step.

7. Keep adding in your broth, 1/2 cup at a time, and gently stirring as it slowly absorbs into the rice. Careful attention and stirring are necessary at this point, so hide your cell phone if you think

you might be interrupted. Focus on stirring and adding the broth until it's gone, and then, within about 25 or 30 minutes, the risotto is just about done. The extra broth should give it a creamy consistency, as the starch content of the rice will thicken it up rather like gravy. Note: if it's a little dry, you can add some more water, and you don't have to add all the broth if you see a consistency that you like—that part's up to you!

8. At this point, it's time to carefully stir in your mushrooms and chicken so that they're well-distributed through your risotto, and then you can stir in your parmesan cheese, sprinkle and stir your parsley, and let it sit on low heat for a few more minutes. Your Italian risotto is ready to serve!

9. Add some more parmesan before serving, and it should be just about perfect. Once you get this recipe down, pick up some pecorino at the store and use it as a substitution as I recommended earlier in the chapter. Pecorino is a sharp Italian cheese made with sheep's milk and grated up to replace the parmesan. It can give you a risotto with a sharp, vibrant flavor!

Homemade Skillet Pizza—A Personal Pizza for One or Two

Everyone loves a good pizza—after all, you can personalize it to your heart's content. Little extra touches like garlic butter or homemade ranch dressing to dip the pieces in (and I'll tell you how to make that ranch later) can really tweak the flavor profile to ten.

Once you've got the basics down, you can even get fancy prepping toppings ahead of time (sautéing mushrooms in butter and wine, for instance...you get the idea!) so that this one simple recipe can be eventually tweaked into a perfect ten that everyone will be begging you to make!

This pizza takes just under two hours to make but don't panic—about an hour and a half of that is prepping your dough and letting it sit—and after that, you're looking at fifteen minutes of prep time and another ten minutes to actually cook it!

Give it a try, and you'll see for yourself—cooking from scratch has never been so easy and rewarding!

Ingredients:

Yeast prep (5 to 10 mins)

- 1 ¼ cups hot water (100–110 degrees Fahrenheit—this is important)
- 2 1/4 tsp active dry yeast
- 1 tsp sugar

Dough

- 3 cups whole wheat or all-purpose flour (keep a little extra to dust your dough)
- 1 tsp salt
- 1 tbsp olive oil

Sample toppings (to get you started with the basics)

- grated provolone, mozzarella, or any comparable cheese substitution you like (you can play with Monterrey Jack or mild cheddar later, for instance)
- pizza sauce (jarred for learning purposes; learn to make YOUR OWN later)

- Parmigiano Reggiano (grated and added to taste)
- basil leaves (fresh, add to taste)

Steps to make:

1. The first step to this recipe is the most important one—you're going to need to activate your bread yeast. You'll do this by mixing your sugar, yeast, and hot water together in a bowl, but I recommend checking the water with a thermometer FIRST—it needs to be 100–110 degrees Fahrenheit. Stir your yeasty ingredients together, and they should be bubbling up and foaming within 5 to 10 minutes.

2. Get your flour and salt into a mixing bowl and pour in your yeasty water, stirring it up nicely with a wooden spoon as you do. Once it's mixed and doughy, you can knead it right on top of the counter as long as it's clean—otherwise, a pastry cloth is the best way to go. I just clean up the counter ahead of time with a little dish soap and water, but any food-safe cleaner will do (Bar Keepers Friend is popular in a lot of kitchens.)

   Note: If your dough is a little bit on the stick side, you can add flour, but do so slowly—one tablespoon at a time. When the dough is ready, it should be smooth, and if you press a finger into it, the indent should push right back up!

3. Once your dough is springy but smooth, go ahead and roll it into a ball and oil it up with your olive oil. After that, stick it in a big bowl and wrap some plastic wrap over it, and then stick it in the cupboard or inside of your microwave and let it sit for an hour and a half.

4. When it's ready, your dough ball will be about 3 times the size that it was before—yay, yeast! At this point, we're good to go with the dough once you take off the plastic cover and push down in the middle of the dough ball to get it to "deflate." Once done, divide it up into 4 pieces and roll each one into a ball.

5. Give each of these balls a dusting of flour, and then you can either stretch out your pizza shape out of each, or if you're not confident with that, you can roll them into circles with your handy rolling pin. Get them as flat as you can and stick them on a large, flour-dusted baking dish or a large, clean, and flour-dusted kitchen towel.

6. Preheat your skillet to medium-high, set your oven to broil, and prep a baking sheet with some parchment paper—it's time to get your toppings and make this pizza. You'll do this by putting one of your flattened doughs into the skillet, immediately smoothing on some pizza sauce so that it's evenly distributed but leaves a little space at the borders for the crust.

7. Sprinkle on your grated cheese next, and scatter your toppings over that. Check your pizza by gently lifting it with the spatula—we're looking for the bottom to char, and when that happens, transfer it to your baking sheet and put it on the middle rack.

8. Be very careful at this point not to overcook your pizza—we just want to melt the cheese to perfection, so 3 to 5 minutes should do it. Once the cheese is melted then take your pizza out, sprinkle it lightly with basil, and you're ready to take your pizza cutter to it for slicing and serving it up!

Chunky Homemade Applesauce—A Delicious Dessert You Can Whip Up on the Fly!

Applesauce is a classic dessert, and it's not all that hard to make. While this recipe calls for McIntosh apples, this is definitely something you can play with—Cortland, Gala, Granny Smith, and Golden Delicious apples are also pretty yummy, and each brings their own unique flavor profile to the table to play with.

Once you've made it a time or two, you'll see for yourself how easy it is, and I highly recommend having some fun with it. Grated ginger and a little cayenne pepper can kick things up and give you something sweet, spicy, and memorable, and you can also play with the sweeteners that you choose (buckwheat honey, for instance, can give it a flavor a little like molasses).

Serve it up with ice cream or on the side with dinner, and don't forget to freeze what you've got left in ice trays—popping the cubes into Ziplocs where they'll freeze nicely and stay good for up to six months! Not bad for a low-maintenance dessert option, no?

This recipe takes a mere thirty minutes to make and yields five servings of applesauce.

Ingredients:

- 3 lb. McIntosh apples (approximately 7 medium-sized apples)
- 1/4 teaspoon vanilla extract
- 1/2 cup sugar
- 1/2 cup water

- 1 tbsp lemon juice

- 1/2 to 1 tsp of cinnamon (try 1/2 first and see what you think)

Steps to Make:

1. First things first, you're going to want to clean the apples. Peel and core them, cutting them up into 8 wedges each. Next, cut those wedges in half crosswise and then toss them into your saucepan.

2. Add in the rest of your ingredients, giving it a quick stir or two with a wooden spoon, and then it's time to turn on the heat. We want to bring the pot contents to a brisk boil, before reducing the heat to a simmer. Your kitchen is going to start smelling like apples very soon, so brace yourself for a treat—the apple and cinnamon aroma is quite heavenly!

3. Let your apples cook for 15 to 20 minutes, stirring them occasionally to avoid surprises, and they should soften right up nicely to your favored consistency. Your homemade applesauce is ready to go!

One extra perk from this recipe is that you can use bruised, ugly apples if you like, so if you keep them fresh at home, then keep that in mind or you can get some less-than-perfect apples at your local farmer's market and make up a big batch to freeze. After that, you can just pop some of those cubes you've frozen and bagged into a sealable plastic bowl and by lunchtime, there's cold, yummy applesauce to compliment whatever's in the lunchbox! Little touches like that are the stuff that nostalgia is made of, so just keep that possibility in mind and do with it what you like!

Delicious DIY Ranch Dressing—Take Your Snacking to the Next Level

Ranch dressing is delicious on salads, but let's face it—for dipping, it's also pretty hard to beat. You can go the healthy route, dipping baby carrots in ranch to enjoy the crunch and flood of tangy flavor, or get a little more decadent and dip your chicken wings in it—it's pretty versatile stuff.

A big problem with families can be keeping up with the demand, and so these little recipes can be an ace up your sleeve to do a little mindful and creative work in the kitchen that will definitely be appreciated.

This recipe also gives you an excuse to expand your spices if you haven't already, and what you'll be getting in the end is a homemade mix that you can convert into either the dressing or a proper dipping ranch that you and your loved ones are going to love.

Best of all, it only takes five minutes to mix up, and if you put it in an airtight glass jar in a cool, dry place, then your mix will be good for up to a month!

With that said, let's take a look at how to make your own homemade ranch mix!

Ingredients:

- 1/2 cup dry buttermilk powder
- 3 tbsp dried parsley
- 1 tbsp granulated garlic
- 2 tsp dried dill
- 2 tsp granulated onion

- 1 tsp dried chives

- 1 tsp kosher salt

- 1 tsp dried onion flakes

- 1/2 tsp granulated sugar

- 1/2 tsp ground black pepper

Steps to Make:

1. Possibly the easiest recipe on the list; no cooking here is needed—simply take the powdered ingredients in their measured amount and whisk them up well together in a bowl. Take a little time while you do, get a good whiff of each ingredient, and familiarize yourself with how the dried spices look. You can even wet your finger, dab it in the mix, and take a quick taste—there's no need to rush, and familiarizing yourself with your kitchen spices really pays off down the line.

2. Carefully spoon out your newly mixed contents into a glass jar to store away for later, or use one of the sections below to make some dip or dressing to enjoy!

Whipping Up Ranch Dip

What you'll need:

- 2 tbsp of your homemade ranch mix

- 16 oz of sour cream

Steps to Make:

1. Add your sour cream to a mixing bowl, and mix in your 2 tablespoons of ranch mix. Be sure to mix it up nice and thoroughly, with a whisk or a kitchen tablespoon and some attitude, and then spoon your dip into a sealable plastic container and stick it in the fridge.

2. Let it chill to perfection (about 1 hour), and your homemade ranch dip is ready to go!

Delicious Dressing, Anyone?

What You'll Need:

- 1/2 cup of whole milk
- 1/2 cup of mayonnaise
- 1 tbsp of your homemade ranch mix

Steps to Make:

1. In a mixing bowl, whisk together your milk, mayonnaise, and homemade ranch mix until you've got a smooth consistency, and that distinctive ranch scent is starting to make you hungry.

2. Carefully pour your ranch into the sealable and airtight container of your choice, using a spoon to make sure that you don't waste any. Refrigerate your dressing for at least 30 minutes, and it's ready to serve up on salads, used in recipes, or whatever else you fancy doing with your ranch!

3. While there is no cooking involved with this particular recipe, don't be too surprised if this is one that you get asked to make a lot—ranch seems to be quite popular these days—and in any case, it also gives you an excuse to teach the recipe to someone special and thus "Give the gift of ranch!"

4. Kidding aside, this recipe is one that improves by simply adding more of what's already in it, although you can try extras like adding lemon zest if you want to personalize your ranch dip or dressing.

Fresh ingredients can also make a difference, but you've got what you need now to discover what you can do on your own. So, try the recipe, and if you like it, then get mindful with it and start playing and learning in your kitchen—it's definitely worth your while!

Bonus Mindfulness Exercise: Miracle Fruit!

This little mindful eating exercise is something that is really fun to share with the whole family. If you've never heard of miracle fruit, it's a West African shrub that produces some amazing little red fruits that have the almost magical property of making sour things taste sweet!

Don't worry—you won't need to import these exotic fruits. Instead, tablets are readily available online, with Amazon being one of the quickest ways to find them. Once they come in the mail, you've got the makings for a truly amazing little mindful eating experiment that I detail below.

What You'll Need:

- miracle fruit tablets

- lemons, limes, grapefruit, and other sour foods

How It's Done:

When you let the miracle fruit tablet dissolve on your tongue, this concentrated form of the West African fruit starts to work its magic almost right away. For the next fifteen minutes to two hours, your taste buds will perceive sour flavors as sweet ones—giving you a new way to explore many foods you've long been familiar with in new ways.

Lemons taste a little like lemonade, grapefruit goes from grim to great, and anything else that's normally sour is going to taste sweet instead. The only rule that you'll want to put in place is to limit the amount of acidic citrus that you eat to a minimum—they'll taste so amazing that it's easy to overdo it, and all that acid will give you a stomachache later.

I recommended preparing a platter with some small samples of the different foods that you want to try. You can include things like shot glasses with a little buttermilk or lemon juice, along with sliced fruits, and whatever else you would like to try.

Discuss the flavors together and savor every moment—this is a unique mindful eating exercise that everyone will definitely remember fondly. As a bonus, it also opens up the subject of making family taste-testing events into a thing—so that everyone gets in the habit of slowing down and enjoying the unique flavors that we've grown of late to take so much for granted.

Chapter Four

Act with Kindness

You might think that little acts of kindness go unnoticed, but nothing could be further from the truth. I think the media is largely to blame for this—whatever channel you turn to, we get to see the worst in people. Shootings, corruption, affairs…Don Henly was basically right—we have an unhealthy fascination with "dirty laundry," and the news knows it.

It's a shame because small acts of kindness might seem like they don't have an impact, but science is proving again and again that this is not the case. In this chapter, I share some little things you can do to have an impact at home for yourself and your loved ones, as well as talk about some studies that have shed light on what kind of impact random acts of kindness can really have.

It's nothing short of amazing!

How Little Things Can Lighten Up Your Entire Day

When you get right down to it, the little things are EVERYTHING, and like your morning coffee, they can sometimes be the fuel that carries you through what would otherwise be a long and difficult day. A good example to remember is those times when you woke up to the smell of cooking breakfast.

Maybe your Mom or Dad liked to cook, or one or both of your grandparents, and every day before school, you could smell the scents coming in from the kitchen well before the alarm reminded you that a new day was afoot. If you grew up with that, it's one of those things that you'll happily reminisce about for the rest of your life!

If you've ever lived in the country, the sound of the morning birds is another pretty thing to wake up and notice, and believe it or not—on a farm, you can get used to the sound of a rooster in the distance, crowing in the dawn with the promise of a productive present.

Little things, especially when tied with nature, really pack a punch when it comes to positive motivation and overall psychological well-being.

For some of us, the sounds of family getting up in the morning can be a sweet but hectic ritual, and it's often the stuff of nostalgia years down the line. I don't know about you, but my family liked to get up a little early, so some unrushed conversation at the breakfast table was always a thing.

While getting up early sounds like a hassle, spending a little family time and talking about the day ahead was something that I grew to love. Looking back, it's kind of funny—an extra 20–30 minutes in the morning took some getting used to, but the trade-off comes in precious mile-markers of morning stories that I wouldn't have had otherwise.

There are little things that you can do now to brighten up your morning with a little kindness and positivity that can make an enormous difference in your days. Here are just a few examples off the top of my head that can sweeten up your days a bit (and get your creative juices flowing to craft a few of your own!):

- **Nature's alarm clock:** Parting the drapes slightly or cracking the blinds before the lights go out can help to make sure that you get some nice, natural sunlight coming into your home early to literally brighten up your day. It's much nicer than the filament bulb eye assault that we thrust on ourselves in the morning and can really help to make sleep feel more like the natural cycle that it is—rather than the rat race routine being forced upon us.

- **On time is LATE:** Getting up a half hour early is a good idea, and one work practice that you should try is ensuring that you're always twenty to thirty minutes early. While this sounds like a drag, it's actually quite empowering! You'll always be on time, and before you jump into the grind, you'll have plenty of time to peek at what you have ahead of you, sip some coffee, catch up on the news, and chat with other early birds in the office. You'll also start your workday fully alert and ready, and believe it or not, your boss will notice that you're always there early, and that really pays off in dividends down the line.

- **Prepping for Friday:** This is something you can do every day or just in preparation for an easy Friday before your precious weekend. Plan things so that you have an easy morning the next day—have your clothes waiting, whip up a yummy breakfast you can quickly reheat the next day, and lay out something at the table to read with it. Simply put, consider the pesky things that you normally do every morning and do as many of those things the night before your "special day." It makes that morning special and really gives you an attitude jump on your day!

- **Morning playlist:** Alarm clocks and phone apps that can play your favorite tunes are easy to get and can make waking up so much better! Music activates the right hemisphere of your brain—which is where your creativity nestles—so this little habit change is not only a pleasure, but it will get your problem-solving gears in motion for the glorious day ahead!

- **Breakfast duty:** If you live with someone else, then trade off morning cooking duties so that at least one day a week, each of you is waking up to the smell of a yummy breakfast. It's a delight, even if whoever doesn't cook gets to do the dishes!

- **Invest in GOOD coffee:** Good coffee is worth it, and you should consider spending a little extra to get your favorites or even a special coffeemaker if you like your coffee a little on the fancy side. Think about how much you spend at the coffee shop for how little you get, and it just makes sense—you'll save money, and you won't have to leave the house and wait in line to get your morning wake-me-up brew of choice! Did I mention that there are coffee makers that can be set to brew before you wake so that the heavenly scent of your favorite fresh, hot coffee is waiting for you? It's SO worth it!

- **The emperor's journal:** Roman emperor Marcus Aurelius had an interesting little trick that he used to do with his journal every morning. He wanted to be a good emperor and knew that he would have to deal with people all day and that the odds were pretty good that some, if not most of them, were going to make him angry. So, he would get up early, write down these people in his journal, and plan to forgive them in advance. It's funny, but it works—for some reason, knowing you'll be speaking to that jerk Mike in the office and that you've forgiven him in advance has a way of making those irritating conversations almost amusing. It's like putting on armor, really, and I highly recommend that you try this.

These are just a few examples of some small kindnesses that you can do for yourself or for the family, but it's a good idea to take a notebook and brainstorm a few things of your own. If you have a family, you can have a little extra fun with it and help the kids build some mindful habits in the meantime with a simple "Family morning" vote.

Get a hat and let everyone make three morning suggestions, each on a piece of paper, and stick them in the hat so that another family member can draw one out. Do this for everyone's threes (or fold them and color the paper and draw one of each color), and then for the next week, everyone gets one thing they want in the morning.

You get the idea—mindful mornings aren't difficult, and they can really transform your week. Not only that, but there's science to back it up!

Little Acts of Kindness Make Big Waves—And Science Backs This Up

When you do something kind for another human being, that warm, toasty feeling that comes with it is actually a chemical called oxytocin. It's quite interesting what it does in the human body and what can kick off an oxytocin flood.

As far as its effects on the body, this chemical is actually good for heart health, as it promotes the release of nitric oxide in your body that expands blood vessels for more efficient blood flow and heart health. It's also important in bonding—a new mother's oxytocin levels have a direct impact on a developing bond with a baby.

If you have a dog or a cat, another fascinating thing about oxytocin is that cuddling with that cat or petting your dog (or even just looking into its eyes for a few seconds!) can also stimulate the production of this bonding chemical—in both you and the animal!

Kindness can do even more than that, and studies performed all over the world that consistently find that a little consideration for yourself and others really DOES go a long way. In the following section, I share a few studies with you that you can check out on your own and you can see for yourself that kindness is good for everyone involved, not just because it's the right thing to do. Our bodies actually respond in measurable ways.

Acts of Kindness Actually Reduce Daily Stress and Can Help Stop Dangerous Cycles

Dr. David A. Fryburg published a study[9] in the *American Journal of Lifestyle Medicine*, which was focused on chronic stress and, more specifically, how acts of kindness and caring tend to promote interpersonal connection, inclusion, and generosity for both parties involved.

This, in turn, had physical effects—especially neurobiological—that produced some concrete data, which Dr. Fryburg discusses in his study. One particularly interesting study that he looked at was titled "A Randomized Controlled Trial of Postcrisis Suicide Prevention."[10] Published in 2001, this study identified 3,005 patients from nine different psychiatric facilities located in San Francisco, California. These patients were severely depressed—in many cases, suicidal and as suicide rates were observed to be the highest for those who refused follow-up treatment within the first two years, the doctors divided these patients into two groups. One group would only receive the usual follow-up letters from the medical facilities upon being discharged from the facility, and the other group would receive more frequent contact in the form of letters from

---

[9] David A. Fryburg, "Kindness as a Stress Reduction–Health Promotion Intervention: A Review of the Psychobiology of Caring," *American Journal of Lifestyle Medicine* 16, no. 1 (Jan–Feb 2021): 89–100, https://doi.org/10.1177%2F1559827620988268.

[10] Jerome A. Motto and Alan G. Bostrom, "A Randomized Controlled Trial of Postcrisis Suicide Prevention," *Psychiatric Services* 52, no. 6 (2001): 828–833, https://doi.org/10.1176/appi.ps.52.6.828.

the staff person who had interviewed them. The letters were simple and always different, but basically, to the effect of "Dear _____, It has been a while since you visited us here at the hospital. We wanted you to know that we hope you are well, and if you'd like to drop us a note to that effect, we'd be happy to hear from you!"

Letters were sent for five years—starting with once a month for the first four months, then every two months for the next eight months, and every three months for the remaining four years. Although only 25 percent of those patients sent letters in response, the doctors checked mortality rates at five, ten, and fifteen years, and the results were pretty stellar. Patients who had received letters asking if they were OK had a significantly higher chance of survival, especially in the first two years, where the mortality rate for those not contacted was twice as high as those who were, and with those contacted, the effects lasted up to fourteen years before they returned to the same risk level as the no contact group of patients.

It's pretty amazing—the occasional letter asking how they were helped save lives for almost a decade and a half!

Dr. Fryburg assessed many studies, looking to identify primary stress factors and data he could find as to how they affected mental and physical health. The key factors he boiled them down into for his own study included:

- healthcare costs

- workplace stress

- financial issues

- discrimination

- loneliness

- bullying
- lack of purpose

These were the most recurring factors that contributed to inducing stress, which resulted in sympathetic nervous system activation and physical symptoms, such as lowered immune response. Prolonged periods of these, in turn, have effects on mental health, physical health, and behavior.

Mentally, issues such as anxiety, cognitive decline, and sleep disorders were some examples of common stress-induced factors, while physical factors like the acceleration of heart disease, asthma, diabetes, and slower healing could also come into play. Behaviorally, this stress also contributed to reliance on stimulants, such as alcohol, drugs, and cigarettes, and behavioral changes included increased temper.

Next, the doctor wanted to see what kind of impact kindness had on these identified stressors and their frightening effects. For the study, kindness was a blanket term meant to encompass prosocial behaviors and emotions—empathy, generosity, caring, compassion, and gratitude. What he found was pretty amazing. Positive social connections show a pattern of an approximately 50 percent reduction in early mortality rates, and multiple studies he cited showed improved cardiovascular health, immune response, and better behavioral habits such as proper diet, exercise, and socialization.

What's more, just as the stressors described create their own "cycle of doom," the data seemed to indicate that prosocial behavior in the form of empathy and kindness tended to create a "virtuous" cycle of its own—essentially a happiness loop.[11]

---

[11] Lara B. Aknin, Elizabeth W. Dunn, and Michael I. Norton, "Happiness Runs in a Circular Motion: Evidence for a Positive Feedback Loop between Prosocial Spending and Happiness," *Journal of Happiness Studies* 13 (2012): 347–355, https://doi.org/10.1007/s10902-011-9267-5.

It's kind of like the old parable where one person is helped out of a terrible situation and offers to repay their rescuer, only to be told that they could repay the debt by helping three or more other people someday. Kindness begets kindness, but science has also proven another really neat thing—just SEEING an act of kindness or compassion makes ripples or even waves that are expressed through the actions of the viewer.

Even Watching or Reading about Kindness Has an Impact

A study published in 2020 by *Frontiers in Psychology*[12] (to which Dr. Fryburg contributed) looked into the impact that kindness media (or media portrayals of people helping or supporting each other) could have in a pediatric health care setting.

Boiling it down to the basics, health care visits to the doctor or dentist are highly stressful for both patients and providers, and the doctors wanted to see if changing the media would produce a measurable effect. Instead of the regular kids' shows that you see at every clinic, original programming was shown so that everyone was watching acts of kindness, compassion, forgiveness, and other uplifting scenarios.

The participants weren't the children—from a pool of fifty participants, twenty-eight were parents and twenty-two were clinic staff—and everyone who took part in the study was told that they would get a gift card.

A control group was shown the normal media to poll their feelings for comparison, and the results were indeed what the doctors had been expecting—the group that watched the kindness media scored significantly higher for feelings of peace, calm, and gratitude. They were

---

[12] David A. Fryburg et al., "Kindness Media Rapidly Inspires Viewers and Increases Happiness, Calm, Gratitude, and Generosity in a Healthcare Setting," *Frontiers in Psychology* 11 (2020): 581942, https://doi.org/10.3389%2Ffpsyg.2020.591942.

also more generous—at the end of the study, both the kindness media group and the control group got their gift cards and were told they could keep them or donate them to a family in need. Eight-five percent of the kindness media group gave away their cards, compared to only 54 percent from the control group. It's definitely a fine argument in favor of performing random acts of kindness every day. Just SEEING them has a ripple effect on us as a species.

Mental Health Clinicians Are Seeing Promising Results with Other- and Self-Focused Kindness Therapies

The impact of kindness in the medical profession has been so profound that, more and more, it is finding its way into mental health treatment. One study[13] in this regard involved a trial with 289 participants, aged between eighteen and seventy years, who were assigned a set of kindness tasks to perform.

To be eligible, they had to have no existing diagnosis of a mental health disorder but a low to moderate level of well-being that the physician-provided tests indicated a risk for mental illness down the line.

Participants were randomly selected to perform one of the four following instructions:

- Perform five acts of kindness for others one day a week and reflect on it the next day

- Perform five acts of kindness for others one day a week without reflection

---

[13] S. Katherine Nelson-Coffey, Ernst T. Bohlmeijer, and Marijike Schotanus-Dijkstra, "Practicing Other-Focused Kindness and Self-Focused Kindness among Those at Risk for Mental Illness: Results of a Randomized Controlled Trial," *Frontiers in Psychology* 12 (2021): 741546, https://doi.org/10.3389%2Ffpsyg.2021.741546.

- Perform five random acts of kindness one day a week for themselves
- Enter a six-week waiting list and choose their own activity from the above selections (this was the control group)

The results? Well, the two groups that performed five random acts of kindness for others, who then reflected or did not reflect on it afterward, showed significantly improved mental health scores. By contrast, those who were assigned five acts of self-kindness showed some improvement—about in the middle between those performing kind acts for others and those simply waiting to choose their task.

The acts of kindness that were performed were pretty basic, even though they had a big impact on mental health. Kind acts could be as simple as saying hi to strangers or giving them compliments, volunteering to help others with chores, or even cash or used items to charity. Acts of kindness for themselves might be having a special movie night with a partner, enjoying some favorite foods or nights out with friends, or a little spontaneous shopping. The top scorer from the study seemed to be "five acts of kindness for others," followed by reflection the next day. This seems to follow the trend that a lot of meditations teach us so that good acts may be reflected upon, and we are inspired to continue and improve upon them.

This is only one particular study, of course, but it demonstrates factually what a lot of us have been trying to tell people for a long time.

A random act of kindness is not a one-sided gift—it improves the lives of everyone involved, and even those lucky enough to see a random act of kindness live and in person!

Ripples in a Pond—The Unseen Impact of Random Acts of Kindness

Random acts of kindness don't have to be overly dramatic to have an enormous impact. The funny thing is that MOST of us don't really believe that, and an article from December 12, 2022, published by *Scientific American*, titled "Kindness Can Have Unexpectedly Positive Consequences,"[14] touched on this odd little quirk that we seem to have regarding small acts of kindness. It cited studies conducted by behavioral scientist Nicholas Epley from the University of Chicago Booth School of Business. Epley's research showed that this "little things aren't important" attitude really seemed prevalent among most people who participated in the studies.

In one study, participants were given cups of hot cocoa to hand out to people at a skating rink and asked to describe their experience, as well as what they expected recipients to do and how "big" they thought the kindness act rated. The people giving out the cocoa predominantly thought that the act was pretty trite and trivial—it's winter, people are skating, and cocoa just kind of "goes" with the experience. The people who had the cocoa were also polled and were pretty thrilled to get delicious hot cocoa on a cold winter day!

Other studies included writing little notes to loved ones to show that you care and giving out free cupcakes. In both instances, participants underestimated the impact that their thoughtfulness and gifts of cupcakes really had—it was kind of funny. That's because participants had been polled in advance to ask how they would like to get a free cupcake for taking part in a quick study, and when their responses were compared to

---

[14] Amit Kumar, "Kindness Can Have Unexpectedly Positive Consequences," *Scientific American*, December 12, 2022, https://www.scientificamerican.com/article/kindness-can-have-unexpectedly-positive-consequences/.

the people who received the free cupcakes from them later, the enthusiasm was almost exactly the same. Giving out the cupcake didn't feel like a big deal, yet the same person was excited about possibly getting one.

We tend to forget that a small kindness, a surprisingly warm act in this chaotic world that we live in, is one of those things that really restores your faith in humanity and gives you a morale boost that can last a day or even longer.

Try to keep this in mind always—the little things really are everything, and when you brighten one person's day, their newly sunny outlook means that you're very likely brightening that same day for everyone else they meet.

Parenting with a Kind Mind

One final study on the impact of kindness on others comes from *Frontiers in Psychology* and was published in 2022. It's titled "Parenting with a Kind Mind: Exploring Kindness as a Potentiator for Enhanced Brain Health,"[15] and the aim of the study was to see if kindness education could help parents manage stress and provide increased empathy and social tools for kids in such situations. The program was a five-module kindness training program called Kind Minds with Moozie, where a cute cow named Moozie would share creative exercises with parents and their three–five-year-old kids so that they could do them together and learn more about kindness—to themselves, others, animals, and the Earth.

Both the parents and children did indeed benefit from the courses supplied in the study, with tests showing improved resilience in the parents and increased empathy in the kids, but more research is definitely

---

[15] Maria Teresa Johnson et al., "Parenting with a Kind Mind: Exploring Kindness as a Potentiator for Enhanced Brain Health," *Frontiers in Psychology* 13 (2022): 805748, https://doi.org/10.3389%2Ffpsyg.2022.805748.

needed. That's because the empathy levels of the kids were still a bit below normal, and the scientists running the tests have a pretty good idea why. This particular testing was going on during the COVID-19 outbreak. With the kids unable to safely socialize, the baseline levels of empathy were pretty skewed. Still, both the parents and the kids did drastically improve their scores, which is indicative that their cognitive abilities were indeed enhanced. Negotiating stress and being more empathetic to others is a skill that requires a certain amount of cognitive flexibility. With stress, you need to be able to stay calm and consider all options, while empathy requires considering other perspectives.

Needless to say, I'll be keeping up with the studies on Kind Minds with Moozie to see where it goes, and if you'd like to learn more, you can visit Moozie.org to check it out for yourself.

Mindfulness Exercise: The Duck Meditation

I wanted to include a mindfulness meditation that the parents out there could share with their kids, and so here we are with the duck meditation.

First and foremost, be sure not to do this with bread—you'll probably get yelled at by other locals if you do. While ducks absolutely love the stuff, nutritionally, it's a bust, so I include a recipe for something healthier that's more like what they eat on their own—basically grains and healthy veggies.

Feeding the ducks can be a great learning experience and a good way to sneak a little mindfulness practice in for your kids. After all, what kid doesn't like feeding the ducks?

I'll provide you with an example of how this might go, but feel free to tweak the exercise to your liking or to otherwise build on it. You might get the kids in the habit of noticing detail, for instance, by asking about the different color patterns on the ducks, having the kids pick out their favorite sounds, or asking them what the pond or surroundings smell like to get them to check and notice—you get the idea.

That said, let's take a look at the meditation, and what you do with it after that is totally up to you!

What You'll Need:

- duck mix (recipe below)
- snacks and beverages for you and the kids (great time to pack a picnic, hint hint!)
- an old blanket for a comfy place to sit

Homemade Healthy Duck Mix:

- 2 cups oats
- 2 cups chopped lettuce or spinach
- 1 cup brown rice (uncooked)
- 1 small plastic bag with assorted small or cut veggies (corn, peas, and carrots are good, but check any veggies you want to include online first to make sure they're safe for ducks)

How It's Done:

1. So that the kids won't get hungry or thirsty, it's best to start off with your impromptu picnic or lunch, so spread out the blanket and get everyone to eat, and then we're ready to start with a quick breathing exercise.

THIS MINUTE MATTERS: THE ESSENCE OF PRESENCE

2. While I'd normally recommend using your favorite breathing exercise, since we're doing this with the kids, we're going to use a kid-friendly modified version of a basic three-three-three breathing technique. Tell the kids to think of something that made them laugh that day and tell them to breathe in through their noses for a count of three —seeing the thing that made them laugh as blue air going into their noses. Tell them to hold that breath for a count of three, so that their imagination can turn that blue color into all the colors of the rainbow. Finally, tell them to exhale for a count of three and imagine the rainbow going out into the world.

3. Do this a few times until the kids feel comfortable doing it on their own, and we're ready to start the exercise.

4. Tell the kids to look at the ducks, paying attention to how gracefully they swim. Ask them which duck they think is the most graceful and ask them to then remember the last time that they were swimming. Did they swim so gracefully? The ducks are so good at such a hard thing because they practice every day, teaching us that we can be graceful in the things that we do if we are willing to work hard enough at them.

5. Have each person reach into the veggie bag to get a single item and tell everyone to throw it in the pond to a different place where a duck can see it.

6. Tell them, "When you do a small kindness for one duck—or one person—then you make them a little happier for the whole day."

7. Tossing a handful of oats, say something like, "When you do a lot of small kind things, the effect is even bigger. Those things don't have to be big—the oats are tiny—so you could do little things

like saying hello to other kids who look lonely, share some snacks with a friend at lunch, or give someone a compliment—use your imagination to try to make them smile. At the end of the day, all those little things add up, like these oats, and like the happy ducks, everyone around you can benefit from your small acts of kindness."

8. Ask the kids if they notice any ducks that didn't get much food and act like you aren't sure which ducks they mean so that they can describe the colors of that duck and the ducks around them.

9. Tell the kids, "Sometimes you'll see someone who needs your help more than any of the others, like that duck you showed me there who can't swim as fast as the others to the food. Whenever you can, try to notice when someone needs your kindness more than others, so that you will know the best place to put it." Have everyone grab a small handful of feed and try to throw it to the unlucky duck.

10. Usually that unlucky duck will still only get a little, but more than they would have without your efforts, so say next to the kids, "That won't always work, of course—you see how sometimes the other ducks still get his snack, but if you look closely, you can also see that SOME of the ducks swim more slowly to help the others. The lesson here is that if your kindness goes to many places in many small ways—just like this handful of duck food—then your kind actions can make the day better for everyone around you."

11. Tell the kids that they can stop the color-breathing for now (they probably already have, but we have a good start on teaching mindful breathing techniques), and suggest something along the lines of "Let's have a little fun getting rid of the rest of this duck mix" and enjoy the rest of your time with the ducks!

It's a little fun exercise, but if you have a good time, then be sure to build on it and have a little fun with it. Making little lessons out of kind acts plants a seed in young minds that can have a great impact on cognitive development. Seeing things from someone else's point of view, in this case, the various ducks, takes little mental gymnastics and gets the kids into a good habit that will help them socially and with problem-solving eventually down the line!

Mindfulness Exercise: The Rain

Another gem of wisdom is that there's a little quote that is often attributed to Buddha although its true source is unknown. That said, it really hits the nail on the head, and it goes like this:

"As rain falls equally on the just and the unjust, do not burden your heart with judgments—but rain your kindness equally on all."

More often than not, one of the trickiest pitfalls of trying to be kinder to others is that we tend to pick the easy targets. These are usually people whom we already like and have built a rapport with. It's an easy mistake to make. First, there's no chance of these people rejecting you or wondering about your intentions like a stranger might. Second, they're in your comfort zone, as they are people that you regularly interact with.

The problem, though, is that once we've done these "easy" acts of kindness, there's a tendency to feel like we've earned kindness "credit," which results in ignoring others whose day you could brighten with a smug attitude of "I've done my good deeds for the day." Kindness is not about that. It's not something that you do to feel better about yourself or to get attention and a reputation for being kind. It's something you do to make someone's day a little brighter.

Yes, it feels good, and you shouldn't feel guilty about enjoying that, but like the rain, your kindness needs to fall on everyone; otherwise, you might "dirty" it a little with insecurity, ego, or, on some level, perhaps a little insincerity.

This exercise will help you to keep centered and remind you to be kind to everyone. Also despite the wary eye that society these days seems to cast on kindness that asks nothing in return, there's nothing wrong with it, and everything is RIGHT.

What You'll Need:

- a comfortable place to sit
- incense (optional)
- light music (optional)
- blanket (if doing this working outside)

How It's Done:

1. Seat yourself comfortably in your apartment or peaceful little nook in nature and start on your breathing exercises to get in a relaxed state and proper frame of mind. You can use your favorite breathing exercise or simply breathe in for a count of three, hold that breath for another count of three, and exhale for a count of three until you feel relaxed and no longer need to count to sustain this rhythm.

2. Visualize a warm, bright light, starting from the core of your body and becoming a pillar straight into the sky. Imagine a small, fluffy cloud forming high above you and imagine the feel of a warm, cleaning rain falling down.

3. Think of the people who you have been kind to this week or even simply the day before, and see them standing next to you,

looking up joyously into the rain. Name each of them aloud or to yourself in your mind, and say what small act of kindness you gave to them. Think about your motivations as you do so—was it something that you did just to brighten their day, or was it for another reason, such as maintaining an ally in the office or because someone else was watching?

4. If you find that your kindness was motivated by anything other than a desire to be kind to others, see that person moving out of your rain and looking sad in the dry spaces beside you. Consider next who else you met during that time period and if there was anything you could have done to brighten their day. This doesn't have to be complicated—a compliment on someone's wardrobe, if you mean it, certainly counts, or asking genuinely about their day.

5. In your visualization, see these people outside of the rain as well, and take a moment to ask each of them what small thing you could have done to brighten their day.

6. Your own creativity and intuition will give them a voice, and as each one tells you a small thing that you could have done, thank them and promise that next time you'll try to remember. As you do, see each of them smiling and disappearing until you are left alone with those whom you were truly kind to for that week or previous day.

7. Let go of the visualization and contemplate what you have learned with a promise to repeat this exercise once a week.

Done regularly, this exercise can help you to truly see the scope of your kindness, so that you can avoid being selective or falling into the trap of going for easy targets where the intent becomes less about kindness and more about worrying about what other people will think of it.

By always questioning your motivations, you will help keep yourself on track, and in time, any insecurities about allowing yourself to be kind in public should fade away. Like the rain, your kindness will flow over all without any bias or hidden motives—and if you'll excuse the pun, that's the genuine kind!

Mindfulness Exercise: A Week to Listen and Learn

Listening is one of those rare skills that can be truly invaluable throughout your life. It is also one of those things that can help make sure that mindfulness doesn't end up moving into self-centeredness.

Let's say that you were in a pine forest. There's a little bit of a chill but a pleasant one—just enough to make your jacket feel like the peak of comfort. Touching a pine tree's leaves, you can tell that they are a little sticky with sap, and the fragrance smells like Christmas. The twigs crunch underfoot, the birds are singing, and you see some of them in full, glorious cover nearby.

Being mindful when enjoying nature is a lot easier than doing the same with people. For instance, when someone tells you their troubles, we have a tendency to give them advice, often without even gauging their intent— maybe they needed to vent or wanted you to agree that the day they've just described was truly horrible.

One of the most mindful ways to know for sure is simply to listen attentively.

Yet another quote that gets misattributed to Buddha, this little piece of wisdom actually comes from F. Scott Fitzgerald's book *Tales of the Jazz Age*[16]:

---

[16] F. Scott Fitzgerald, *Tales of the Jazz Age* (New York: Bottom of the Hill Publishing, 2014).

THIS MINUTE MATTERS: THE ESSENCE OF PRESENCE

"It's more important to be kind than to be right. Many times, what people need is not a brilliant mind that speaks, but a special heart that listens."

You'll see it a lot in Buddha memes, but that's understandable—this is a very astute observation and certainly worthy of meditating upon and taking to heart.

In this exercise, you're going to take a weeklong vow of "almost silence," and what I mean by that is that you will listen without providing judgments or any opinions unless SPECIFICALLY asked for them.

Your goal is to get the person to talk—so if they ask your opinion, you can try to deflect once with "What did you feel about this?" but if they push, then you can give your opinion—we're just practicing active listening, so there is no need to make things awkward.

What You'll Need:

- eyes and ears
- a comfortable spot at home for evening mediation
- incense (optional for later)
- light music (optional for later)

How It's Done:

1. Active listening requires some basic things that you'll need to practice, but don't worry—it's not overly complicated. You need to give the person your full attention, listen to their words, and also watch their body language.

2. When the person describes things to you, such as events that happened or their feelings, try to repeat what they have told you in your own words every now and again. If you've been listening closely, you'll be able to do this accurately, and the other person's body language and facial expressions will show you that you're on the right track. People feel reassured when you can demonstrate that you are listening, and this is one of the best ways to do it, but if you get it wrong a couple of times, then you don't have to push it. Practice makes perfect, and you've got all week.

3. In the evening, take a little time to meditate on what you've learned listening during the day. Sit in your comfy spot, light up your incense and put your music on if that's your preference, and sit down somewhere comfortable.

4. Begin your favorite breathing exercises or do a simple three-three-three, where you inhale, hold, and exhale for a count of three for each, and when you feel relaxed and the pattern comes naturally to you, then you are ready to visualize.

5. Replay a conversation that you had during that day in your mind, focusing on what you remember them saying, as well as any body language you can remember. Tapping feet, crossed arms, the occasional raised eyebrow—don't worry if you don't know what the body language means yet; just get in the habit of noticing. This is always something you can study later.

6. Think of the responses that you used to the person and ask yourself if you let any personal opinions creep in, any judgments, or if you tried to steer the conversation your way—either toward a conclusion you wanted to infer or even if you tried to hurry the exchange.

7. At this point, you can replay another conversation if you like, but if it's the first time, it's better to stick to one and consider what you have learned. It's not easy to REALLY listen, so if parts of the conversation are vague to you, that's OK—with practice, they won't be!

Try this for a week and see what you can teach yourself about listening—as the days pass, you'll notice that you are remembering more, and believe it or not, you might find the conversations quite a bit richer and much less frustrating than they seemed before.

A little body language study can also come in handy if you are interested in teaching yourself active listening. Books such as *Emotions Revealed: Recognizing Faces and Feelings to Improve Communication and Emotional Life* by Paul Ekman[17] can teach you cues that people broadcast to help you better fully understand what they are saying—and what their bodies are saying, too.

A good listener is a kindness that most of us want but seldom get to enjoy. Not only will you brighten their day, but this is a skill that is very rewarding—it tends to enrich friendships and relationships with significant others, and, of course, there is a final perk. You'll start listening to truly UNDERSTAND rather than simply listening so that you can REPLY, and believe me—the lucky people in your life will notice!

---

[17] Paul Ekman, *Emotions Revealed: Recognizing Faces and Feelings to Improve Communication and Emotional Life* (New York: Holt Paperbacks, 2007).

Chapter Five

Forgive and Let Go

Forgiveness can seem like one of the hardest things on the planet—this is especially true if you are dealing with something from childhood that was powerful enough to send ripples into your present, but a slight doesn't have to be old to be effective. For instance, your child's grandparent might spank your child after you've told them that this kind of discipline is outdated and dangerous, or a close friend might suddenly go "Dr. Jekyll or Mrs. Hyde" on you and betray a confidence that hurts you or someone else more vulnerable.

Let's face it—there are countless ways that those whom we trust can "drop the ball" and do something so vile to us personally that forgiveness seems like a pipe dream, and in this chapter, we're going to go into how dangerous this can be for you and what you can do about it.

The Roman emperor Marcus Aurelius once said that the "best revenge is to be unlike the one who harmed you," and while that sounds like a lofty sentiment for a pampered Roman emperor, it's actually some pretty sound advice for anyone. That's because holding a grudge and withholding forgiveness doesn't just punish the person who wronged you (and arguably, they might not even care!), but it also has a definite impact on you and your ability to enjoy life to its fullest.

The Importance of Forgiveness

An article in *Psychology Today* titled "Forgiveness"[18] tackled the subject nicely and is well worth a read when you have a little free time, although I don't know if I agree with 100 percent of what was said. As for the highlights, they pointed out that when you hold a grudge against someone, your brain gets in the habit of producing a chemical response when you see them or, in some cases, even when you think of their name. As a result, your brain gets a flooding-level dose of adrenaline and cortisol, which can lead to anxiety, and if you are already dealing with a chemical imbalance, such as when diagnosed with bipolar disorder or clinical depression, this unwanted chemical rush can really mess with your senses.

Now it is their opinion that some acts are unforgivable, and that for these, some people find empowerment in giving themselves permission to never forgive that person. If that works for you, then by all means, go with it. However, it is my opinion that these things can be forgiven so that you can move on for one simple reason: Forgiveness does NOT imply acceptance. People do some of the most horrible things to other human beings for reasons that we may understand but, of course, still cannot condone. Perhaps they were physically, verbally, or sexually abused as a child. They may have chemical imbalances in their brains that create violent or otherwise deviant behaviors that they can control no more than a person struggling with alcohol or drug use disorder could control their own addiction.

You can't control this. In some cases, you can't even keep these toxic people out of your life, but what you can control is what you ALLOW into your mind. You've probably heard the phrase "forgiveness is a gift that you give to yourself," and this is 100 percent true, but I think what keeps people

---

[18] Psychology Today, "Forgiveness," accessed May 16, 2024, https://www.psychologytoday.com/us/basics/forgiveness

from giving themselves this gift is that we tend to think that "making up" with the person is the natural act that follows forgiveness.

It can be, but it doesn't have to. You don't have to trust someone after you forgive them. You don't have to let them in your life. Psychologists tend to describe forgiveness as "making the decision to let go feelings of vengeance or resentments directed at a group of people or an individual who has harmed you in some way—whether they deserve it or not."

For instance, you may have made the decision not to be around someone who has harmed you to the point that they've essentially been edited out of your life. That's all well and good, but when someone else in your circle mentions their name, and you immediately become uncomfortable, then your mind is telling you that you need to finish the job.

Epictetus said in the *Enchiridion*, **"Anyone who can anger you becomes your master—they can only make you angry if you PERMIT them to disturb you."** If you can put aside the quick flare of resentment that this quote may have provoked for a moment to think about it, he's right.

YOU are in control of your mind, and while mindfulness is a beautiful thing, this is one of the more advanced aspects of living a mindful life—you need to "clean the house" in your own mind if you wish to fully make every minute matter.

Consider this—how many times has the mention of that person caused you to have a bad day or even a bad weekend, even when you didn't see the actual person? They've already committed whatever act it was that harmed you so and made it part of the immutable past. So the only thing left that you CAN control is your judgment of what happened and, as a result, how much power you will allow it to have hold of you.

It's really about accepting that there are toxic elements in life beyond your control and that these horrible things can and do happen—you're not condoning it, but forgiving the action to complete the total edit you have already started of this person from your life. Like making them a footnote, rather than a chapter or a recurring character in the book of your life. Separate it from the person—you are really just making a conscious decision to not let toxic resentment into your mind. You may also need to take the difficult step of accepting that you may NEVER know the reason why they did it.

You can sometimes fill in the blanks to help yourself move on if that will help you to avoid wasting time on investigating someone's motivations—which are tricky to find at best. If someone robbed you, would you be more inclined to forgive them if they had a sick child at home to feed? A drunk driver who took someone away from you may have had too much to drink at their recently deceased mother's wake. You can invent something convenient if it helps you to forgive, but even if you just decide that you may never know their motivations, and that's OK, then this is something that needs to be done—you're going to have to forgive them as best you can to move on.

Again, none of this makes the wrong into a right—your focus needs to be on doing everything you can to allow yourself to mark this transgression off in your mind as a "tragedy" that you COULD NOT CHANGE.

Interestingly enough, there have been some studies on forgiveness where magnetic resonance was used to watch the brain and compare the areas that lit up when someone has forgiven another and when they have NOT. One study from *Frontiers in Human Neuroscience* titled "How the Brain Heals Emotional Wounds: The Functional Neuroanatomy of Forgiveness"[19] did exactly that. In the study, volunteers were each given a

---

[19] Emiliano Ricciardi et al., "How the Brain Heals Emotional Wounds: The Functional Neuroanatomy of Forgiveness," *Frontiers in Human Neuroscience* 7 (2013): 839, https://doi.org/10.3389%2Ffnhum.2013.00839.

scenario where someone in their life did something horrible to them, and they were instructed to either work out how to forgive them or to think of fun and interesting ways to avenge themselves.

The study found that those who were instructed to find a way to forgive—such as to consider their own part in the problem or those who were told the person who harmed them was mentally ill—showed greater activity in the anterior cingulate cortex, which plays a crucial role in various cognitive functions, including decision-making, empathy, error detection, and emotional regulation. This is very important because that part of your brain regulates emotional stability. By contrast, those who were told to encourage a grudge exhibited more activity in the prefrontal cortex areas of the brain, which regulate aggression, and what's more, these areas tended to flare up with subsequent scenarios. Put simply—those who didn't forgive would keep showing feelings of aggression in unrelated scenarios. You keep carrying that anger around, and it pollutes all of your interactions the moment you think that someone might try to deceive or harm you.

This is why forgiveness is all about YOU—not them—and with the exercises later in the chapter, I'll provide some meditations that can help you get where you need to fully edit these toxic people out of your life so that you can start truly enjoying it.

How Resentments Steal Your Time Away

In order to help drive the lesson home, you need to consider just how much time these old grudges can occupy in your mind and how much they sabotage your chance at having a good life on your terms. For instance, family gatherings can be a great example.

Your parents, siblings, or other relatives are often a source of pain, perhaps from something they have directly said or done to you or even just annoying habits of seeming to judge your life. Immediately upon seeing that person, you're going to get a substantial dose of cortisol and adrenaline from your brain, and guess what?

Every person you talk to is going to get the results. As I discussed in the previous section, the study cited shows that you've not got the areas in your brain that modulate aggressive response lighting up like the Fourth of July.

Stop a moment and compare your interactions with a favorite relative when you are alone with how you speak with them in a crowded family get-together, and you'll see what I mean. Even if you feel relief talking to that person in the crowded family venue, your heart is racing, and you're looking for a threat that you feel you need to squash the entire time. It's taking away from your precious time with the family members you actually like!

After the gathering, you're going to spend time thinking about the person who offended you as well, so that a little of that poison will make you more defensive when you're spending time with your friends or maybe even make you sharp with coworkers or even your boss!

It's essentially a toxic version of mindfulness that you are allowing to travel with you and to influence you day to day, and it's going to keep stealing minutes from you for as long as you let it.

Forgiveness Is a Gift to Yourself: Learning How to Let Go

Now that you know that your brain is actively producing unwanted chemicals to generate anxiety from the grudges that you carry, how do you put a stop to it? Well, you've read this far, so you've already taken the first steps—you realize that grudges carry very real consequences long beyond when they were earned.

By choosing to forgive the ones that have harmed you, you aren't giving a gift to them, but to yourself. The past is immutable and no matter how much we'd like to forget it sometimes, it's there and it simply cannot be changed. We can only change our judgment of it—as if it were an automobile accident that we survived or an illness that we thought might kill us, yet we endured.

Before I give you the forgiveness exercises, I'll leave you with a classic Buddhist story that I've always felt really captured the essence of "how to forgive the unforgivable." It comes from Buddhist monk and author Gelong Thubten,[20] who says that it's a very old and inspiring story that goes something like this:

One day, a Buddhist monk charged with teaching students at his temple came across an angry student. Asking him what was wrong, the boy told him someone threw and subsequently hit him with a stone! The monk looked at the boy, who was rubbing a spot on his head where the stone had struck, and he asked him a curious question: "Who are you so angry with?"

Looking surprised, the boy answered, "I'm angry at the person who threw the stone at me!" The monk then raised a finger and said, "Ahh, but was it not the stone that struck you, causing so much pain? Why are you not, then, truly angry with the stone?"

"The stone could not be responsible for hurting me," said the boy, "it had no good or evil intentions. It could not help being thrown at me by the person whom I am now angry with!"

The teacher smiled at him and said, "Can you not see that by your own logic, this person is not the one who hurt you, but rather it is the pain?"

---

[20] Gelong Thubten, *A Handbook for Hard Times—A Monk's Guide to Fearless Living* (London: Yellow Kite, 2004).

"I don't understand," the boy said, and the monk explained, "Like the stone, the person was also helpless against being thrown...by his own pain."

I hope that you enjoyed that little story, and with that, here are those exercises!

Mindfulness Exercise: Two Handles Meditation

Often the most daunting test of your peace and resolve comes in the form of a family get-together. It makes sense—these are people that you grew up with, who knew their own version of you that may or may not contrast greatly with who you are today.

This usually gives them the ability to push your buttons, but I have something that can help! It's a Stoic technique that you can meditate on and use the next time you need to be around family members or close friends who have a nasty habit of stressing you out!

It comes from the *Enchiridion* of Epictetus,[21] a book whose origins go back to about the second century AD. In this particular passage, Epictetus warns us to be mindful of how we respond to someone. He said:

"Every event has two handles—one by which you can lift it and another by which you cannot. If your brother does you wrong, do not grab at this wrongdoing, for this is the handle that is not strong enough to move it. Instead, use the other—that he is your brother, whom you grew up with, and you will be holding the handle that can surely carry."

This is a powerful observation—oftentimes people in our family are the ones who can hurt us the most, because of the many years that have

---

[21] Epictetus, *Enchiridion*, trans. George Long (Mineola, NY: Dover Publications, Inc., 2004).

been shared together. By the same token, with a little practice with this meditation, you can use that same familiarity to better understand them and to take the sting out of the words.

Epictetus also said, "Anyone who can anger you becomes your master. They can only make you angry if you permit them to disturb you," and we'll incorporate this into the meditation so that you can put this ancient philosophy to good use!

I'll walk you through the steps of the meditation so that you can give it a try and see for yourself—that family familiarity being used to harm you can become the healing foundation for working past your differences.

What You'll Need:

- a comfortable spot where you can be alone and undisturbed
- incense (optional)
- instrumental or otherwise light music (also optional)
- a blanket (if you will be doing this outside)
- a piece of paper with the above quote written on it

How It's Done:

1. Find a comfortable spot at home or outdoors where you won't be disturbed and sit down comfortably. You can put on some music in advance if it helps you to relax and light some incense if you like, but that part is completely optional.

2. Start your favorite breathing exercise, or you can do a simple one by breathing in for a count of three, holding your breath for a

count of three, and exhaling for a count of three. Do this until your breathing assumes this pattern without prompting it, and we're ready for the next step.

3. Say the quote aloud: "Every event has two handles—One by which you can lift it and another by which you cannot. If your brother does you wrong, do not grab at this wrongdoing, for this is the handle that is not strong enough to move it. Instead, use the other—That he is your brother, whom you grew up with, and you will be holding the handle that can surely carry."

4. Visualize a time when you argued with a family member and lost your temper. Now stop the scene so that the two of you are frozen in your mental picture. Replace the form of the family member with a younger one—visualize them from when they were younger and from a happy memory that you shared together. If you have no shared happy memories, simply visualize them as a child—still related to you, but saying the same words. Do they have the same sting, coming from a petulant child in a young, high-pitched voice?

5. Contemplate this for a moment, and then say aloud, "Anyone capable of angering me becomes my master—they can anger me only if I permit them to do so."

6. Visualize the confrontation scene again, with your family member as a child, and hear the words again without allowing them to control how you feel—like you would when reasoning with an angry child.

7. Contemplate how this event would have been if you had not allowed them to stoke up the fires of your anger. Don't dwell on it too much—this meditation is not about digging up old wounds but about empowering you against new ones.

8. Repeat aloud, "Every event has two handles—One by which you can lift it and another by which you cannot."

Let your breathing return to normal, and be mindful of the impressions that you'll be getting over the next week. While this approach doesn't guarantee that you can sway a family member's opinions or get them to change their habit of trying to push your buttons, it can empower you to better deal with this stress so that it won't leak into your present life.

You can also alternate the visualization, so that the person saying the harmful things to you is someone completely different whose opinions aren't so important to you. This is very useful, as it helps to drive the lesson home that those words cannot harm you unless you LET THEM. You're in control of your mind, after all, and to drive that lesson home, I share a last quote from that wise old philosopher Epictetus and his *Enchiridion*:

"If someone in the street were entrusted with your body, you would be furious! Yet you entrust your mind to anyone around who happens to insult you, and allow it to be troubled and confused. Aren't you ashamed of that?"

When you've learned not to be distracted or harmed by hurtful words, what's left is the perspective to see once again the loved one hiding behind them, and that's the handle that you can carry this with.

Mindfulness Exercise: Putting Critics in Their Place

Whenever you start taking control of your life, there never seems to be a shortage of critics. This can be quite toxic if things go badly—we tend to believe something when we hear it enough—but a Roman emperor who ended his reign over 1,800 years ago had a nice little solution for critics. Marcus Aurelius Antoninus, one of the last good Roman emperors, advised:

"If any man is able to convince me and show me that I do not think or act right, I will gladly change; for I seek the truth—by which no man was ever injured—but he is injured who abides in his error and ignorance."[22]

It basically amounts to "if they're right, be thankful and learn from them," and when you really think about it, he's got a good point. Old Marcus was a student of Stoicism, and that philosophy was all about learning what you can and cannot control so that you learn not to stress over the "cannots," and then dominate every single "can" that you can.

This exercise will help you to put critics in proper perspective—they're either RIGHT, in which case you have a chance to improve yourself and should actually be THANKFUL, or they're WRONG, and the criticism is simply an unfair opinion. Since you can't change an unfair opinion (think about political arguments you've had to get the proper perspective), that's not something you have to stress over.

Just take the good bits and write the bad ones off as things you cannot change, which thus shouldn't concern you. When you can start seeing critics this way, that old chestnut of "nobody likes a critic" will no longer apply to you—you might even hope that someone "cracks wise," just in case there's REAL wisdom in it ripe for the taking!

What You'll Need:

- a comfortable spot to meditate
- incense (optional)
- music (optional)

---

[22] Marcus Aurelius, *Meditations*, trans. James Harris (CreateSpace Independent Publishing Platform, 2016).

How It's Done:

1. Find yourself a comfortable spot. I prefer being out in nature, but if that's not your thing or the local mosquitoes might be a bit too distracting, then you can simply do this inside where you can be sure you won't be disturbed.

2. Sit down and begin your favorite breathing exercise, or go with the standard three-three-three (breathe in for a count to three, hold it for another count of three, and exhale for three whole seconds). Do this until you don't have to think about the count, and then we're ready to meditate.

3. Visualize a time when someone criticized you, and you immediately became defensive. This should be a time when that person's criticism stung particularly because some of the things they said were correct. Focus on your defensive attitude and be honest with yourself. Did it hurt because you felt "reduced" in front of someone whose opinion is important to you? Were you upset because this person was wrong 99 percent of the other times that they spoke, and it was irritating that they were correct this time? Did you feel they were "beneath you" because of the mess they've made of their own lives or that you were being attacked for trying something new?

4. Spend a good, long time thinking about this—if what they said was true, why did you decide to take it as harm? Now recreate the situation in your mind, and instead of the critic you were angry with, visualize the scene with a trusted mentor giving you the same critique in soothing tones—like a favorite teacher. What would you have done with their "truth" in that situation? Would you have wasted time and harmed a personal relationship

fighting that truth, or would you have simply felt a little humbled and then decided that you could benefit from what you heard?

5. Let your breathing return to normal and give yourself the day to contemplate what you've learned at your leisure. Just like how an insult from a family member stings so much more than one from a person you don't care about, criticism can harm us—but only if we DECIDE that we've been harmed. The next time that someone criticizes you, pause and think of the mentoring voice that you substituted in this exercise telling you the same thing. If it rings true—then don't be angry—consider it a teaching moment. You might even tell the person, "You may be right; I'll think about that. Thanks," and go about your merry way. Not only does this completely defuse what might have turned into an altercation that wouldn't improve your life in the slightest, but you've just gotten some great advice that you can use to make yourself or what you are doing even better!

Granted, some people criticize just to be mean, but remember that this advice comes from Marcus Aurelius, whose philosophy said that happiness lies in learning what you can and cannot control. If someone is criticizing you to be mean then that's definitely something YOU can't control, but you can control your perception of it. If there's nothing to learn, it's not worth giving a second thought, and frankly, if they need to criticize you to feel good about themselves, then that kind of dysfunction is more deserving of your pity than the fight they're trying to manipulate you into having with them.

Finally, don't forget that some people are simply socially inept, and what felt like an attack might have been their clumsy way of trying to be helpful. This meditation covers all of those instances.

When you learn to see every critic as a potential chance to get an outside perspective that you might have otherwise missed, then you'll actually start looking for useful quips from those formerly annoying know-it-alls!

While you can just do this mediation once, I recommend giving it a "refresher run" every now and again to remind yourself to stay humble and open to input. One of the pitfalls of successfully adopting a truly mindful attitude is that our egos can get a little inflated, and we start "peeling the layers" and learning more about ourselves. By reminding yourself that wisdom can come from anywhere or anyone, you'll stay humble and keep yourself on the right path!

Mindfulness Exercise: I Am Not the One You Harmed

In many cultures, it is considered that each person is not simply one person but rather a collection of people that are scattered through a timeline. For instance, the Vikings had the fates, also called the Norns, who were named Urðr, Verðandi, and Skuld. This meant "Past," "Present," and "Future," with the lesson being that you are three people—who you were, who you are, and who you are becoming. In Buddhism, there is even a fantastic quote to this effect that comes directly from Buddha himself. It was supposedly something that he said when a man he had quarreled with came to him, after learning that he was Buddha and prostrated himself at Buddha's feet to ask for forgiveness. Buddha would not forgive him, as it was not necessary, because in his eyes, the man had quarreled with "Buddha of yesterday" but was now speaking with the new "Buddha of today." He said to the man:

"And you also are new. I can see you are not the same man who came yesterday because that man was angry and he spit, whereas you

are bowing at my feet, touching my feet. How can you be the same man? You are not the same man, so let us forget about it. Those two people, the man who spit and the man on whom he spit, both are no more. Come closer. Let us talk of something else."[23]

The speaker has a really good point there, and I explain more of this in the meditation exercise so that you can make use of this ancient and multicultural approach. So that you know in advance, if what the person did to you is brutal to the point that you can no longer associate with them, that's OK—this is still workable—and I'll go into that along the way.

What You'll Need:

- a quiet place where you won't be disturbed
- a piece of paper with the above quote written on it
- a favorite incense (optional)
- some instrumental music you like in the background (optional)

How It's done:

1. Find your isolated and quiet space and get comfortable. Where you go is up to you—you can do this indoors and add some incense and low-volume music to help get you in the right mindset, or you could even lay out a blanket somewhere in nature if that's your preference.

---

[23] This one is a subject of contention. While some believe this story was derived from the *Akkoso Sutta*, it is also cited in a book by Osho titled *Intimacy: Trusting One's Self and the Other* (New York: St. Martin's Griffin, 1997). Still, the message is a powerful one, so I'm including this with a little scholarly due diligence for you, readers, courtesy of these footnotes!

2. Sit down comfortably with your paper nearby and begin a simple breathing exercise or use another that you prefer. The simplest is simply a three-three-three—Breathe in for three seconds, hold it for three seconds, and breathe out for another three. Do this until you don't have to think of the count, and you should be relaxed and ready. Recite the quote rewritten below, and feel free to swap the pronouns as needed for yourself and the person you are looking to forgive—I'll keep them binary in the example, and you can simply replace as needed. **"And you also are new. I can see you are not the same man/woman who came yesterday because that man/woman was angry and he/she spit, whereas you are bowing at my feet, touching my feet. How can you be the same man/woman? You are not the same man/woman, so let us forget about it. Those two people, the man/woman who spit and the man/woman on whom he spit, both are no more. Come closer. Let us talk of something else."**

3. Take a moment to contemplate the wisdom behind this. Think first of yourself as a child and who you were then, moving along to your teenage years, and also consider your future potential as it relates to what came before. Consider some things that you learned along the way that helped you change into the person you are today, and the seeds you've planted now that will one day come to fruition. Some of these things were in your control, but others were not, and this is an important distinction—it is the same for the person you are trying to forgive.

4. Consider now the person you wish to forgive, and try to see them the same way—who they were, are, and who they are becoming. This person had their own childhood and teen years and aspects of their life in their control, like yourself, they had many that

were not in their control. Consider that, like you, this person is the product of a constant and evolving transformation—they are not the same person that they were yesterday, nor a decade ago, or even as a child. That past is a part of them, but they are currently a new person—who they are now—and they are their potential—who they will be.

5. Once you have contemplated a more nuanced and realistic view of both yourself and this person as constantly changing entities through your set timelines, then you must consider forgiveness. You CAN forgive them while also choosing never to associate with them. If you are uncertain about whether or not to keep them in your life as they are now, then simply ask yourself, "If this person did _____ again to me, could I handle it, and would I still feel that the time I put into this was worthwhile?" And if the answer is "no," then you have the right answer, just perhaps not the one that you want.

6. Hold the visualization of the both of you in all of your aspects—who you both were, are, and will be—and take a moment to appreciate the enormity of this—What we call a 'soul' isn't a singular entity, but rather a crowd all its own made of the past, present, and future.

7. When you are ready, then see your "selves" looking at the other person's 'selves' and simply say 'I forgive you' or if you have decided that this is someone you need to let go, then say, "I forgive you so that I may move on." As you do, hear the voices of your past and future selves chiming in to say the same words, and when you are ready, let go of the visual and return to normal breathing—you're done unless you want to add the optional next step.

8. Optional: Contemplating the view of your selves, tell the representation of the other person that you are currently visualizing what YOU did to complicate the matter. This won't always apply—sometimes people do things to us that are completely outside of our control—but if the quarrel was of the two-sided kind, then this step is important. Looking upon your past, present, and future selves, ask each of them what they/you brought to the quarrel that you and the other person shared. This part may surprise you—your past selves may say that you brought fears with you from previous traumas that might not even apply to this person, your current self may say that these traumas or fear of what effects they might have on your "now" made you too prideful or frightened to risk talking further, your future selves may say that you never had room for this person in your future in the first place! Take a moment and listen to what each of them has to say—they're you, after all, in all your complex glory. If you decide to work things out with the person directly, then what you hear now in this meditation will be vital for mending the physical relationship.

This is something that you can repeat as needed, with the same person or anyone else that you are having trouble forgiving. If you feel the need to repeat this, however, then you may wish to add the extra optional step.

Above all, remember that forgiveness doesn't mean approval or even that you are keeping that person in your life. It's a gift to yourself, and when you view people as they really are—a complex array of newly created souls across the small or vast timeline they'll encompass—it helps you to put things into perspective. You're essentially forgiving an aspect of them that is long gone for harming a version of you that also passed away long ago. Once you realize this and see the freedom that it gives you to move ahead with your life, the feeling is nothing short of amazing!

Conclusion

I'd like to take a moment before we part ways to thank you for taking this journey with me and to give a quick recap of some of the basics that we've learned here. They boil down to the following essentials that you'll want to practice to ensure that this minute matters!

- **Be There:** Your mind likes to save on "processor power" by taking routine and absorbing as little of it as possible. This costs you so many moments that you could have kept, so it's vital that you practice being fully present in the moment. This will take the dull humdrum of every day and transform it—simply by your determination to take an active role in each and every moment. This, in turn, will help in all aspects of your life—relationships, anxiety, and stress management, and give you the sharp focus of a detective determined to solve the meaning of life!

- **Listen to the Laughter and Smell the Roses:** When you've mastered the art of slowing down and savoring each and every moment, then you're ready to go from "moment glutton" to a "continuance connoisseur." This is done by picking and choosing the moments you wish to extend, and, if you're lucky, bringing some keepsakes with you to savor down the line. An appreciation of this time leads to a better understanding of how time changes things, such as a child's laughter or a tree you've all planted as a family in the front yard. By choosing what to keep, you'll ensure that this minute matters because you've cherry-picked the best in advance!

- **Cook with Love:** Cooking is one of the purest forms of love that you can share, and when you cook from scratch, it's even better! Learning to make different things with whatever is available is a lesson that carries through your entire life, and when you can craft delicious meals specifically for your loved one's favorite tastes, you've got the recipe for a shared minute that truly matters. It's something they'll keep with them for a lifetime and another precious thing you can share. As an added bonus, home cooking is one of the best morale-boosting skills you can develop that makes positive ripples in your family's life, and there are psychology studies that prove it!

- **Act With Kindness:** The little things are everything, and while a small act of kindness might not seem like much, these little acts ripple outwards like a tiny pebble thrown into a still pond. Random acts of kindness invoke a chemical response in both the giver and receiver, and this, in turn, affects how you and those you've been kind to will then go about your day. You aren't just being kind to one person—you're literally sending ripples of kindness out into the world that spread in ways you'll never see but that science proves they are truly profound.

- **Forgive and Let Go:** As they say, "Forgiveness is a gift that you give to yourself." By letting go of grievances, you aren't saying that they were right or justified, nor that you shouldn't have been angry when they occurred. Rather, you are taking an active role by accepting that these grievances are part of the immutable past—something you cannot change—and that by forgiving them, you are simply deciding not to let the pain from these incidents control you and continue to affect your ability to enjoy life to its fullest.

I hope that you will practice the mindful exercises scattered throughout this book to your benefit and don't forget to get a little creative with them—each one makes a fine foundation that you can build on or simply use to inspire you to create meditations of your own.

Take advantage of your developing skills to pick and choose the minutes that you want to keep, and before you know it, you won't have so many blurs in your memory to deal with the next time that someone asks you what you did last week.

Life is only routine when you let it be so. Once you've taken control of it by allowing yourself to notice the vibrant sights, scents, smells, textures, and tastes around you then you'll see the truth for yourself.

This minute matters, and that, my new friends, is the essence of presence.

Now what are you waiting around there for?! Get out now and start living your life your way! Time waits for no one but on the bright side, you've got everything you need now to make the most of it.

This minute matters, so what are YOU going to do with yours? Whatever you decide, I hope that it's glorious!

Bibliography

Aknin, Lara B., Elizabeth W. Dunn, and Michael I. Norton. "Happiness Runs in a Circular Motion: Evidence for a Positive Feedback Loop between Prosocial Spending and Happiness." *Journal of Happiness Studies* 13 (2012): 347–355. https://doi.org/10.1007/s10902-011-9267-5.

Ball, Catherine. "Making Memories Matters, Even If Your Baby Won't Remember Them." *Parents*, August 30, 2023. https://www.parents.com/kids/development/childhood-amnesia-heres-why-your-child-cant-remember-being-a-baby/.

Buddhist Suttas. Translated by T. W. Rhys Davids. Oxford: Clarendon Press, 1881.

Dialogues of the Buddha Volume 2. Translated by T. W. Rhys Davids. London: Henry Frowde, 1910.

Ekman, Paul. *Emotions Revealed: Recognizing Faces and Feelings to Improve Communication and Emotional Life*. New York: Holt Paperbacks, 2007.

Epictetus. *Enchiridion*. Translated by George Long. Mineola, NY: Dover Publications, Inc., 2004.

Farmer, Nicole, and Elizabeth W. Cotter. "Well-Being and Cooking Behavior: Using the Positive Emotion, Engagement, Relationships, Meaning, and Accomplishment (PERMA) Model as a Theoretical Framework." *Frontiers in Psychology* 12 (April 2021): 560578. https://doi.org/10.3389/fpsyg.2021.560578.

Fitzgerald, F. Scott. *Tales of the Jazz Age*. New York: Bottom of the Hill Publishing, 2014.

Fryburg, David A. "Kindness as a Stress Reduction–Health Promotion Intervention: A Review of the Psychobiology of Caring." *American Journal of Lifestyle Medicine* 16, no. 1 (Jan–Feb 2021): 89–100. https://doi.org/10.1177%2F1559827620988268.

Fryburg, David A., Steven D. Ureles, Jessica G. Myrick, Francesca D. Carpentier, and Mary Beth Oliver. "Kindness Media Rapidly Inspires Viewers and Increases Happiness, Calm, Gratitude, and Generosity in a Healthcare Setting." *Frontiers in Psychology* 11 (2020): 581942. https://doi.org/10.3389%2Ffpsyg.2020.591942.

Johnson, Maria Teresa, Julie M. Fratantoni, Kathleen Tate, and Antonia Solari Moran. "Parenting with a Kind Mind: Exploring Kindness as a Potentiator for Enhanced Brain Health." *Frontiers in Psychology* 13 (2022): 805748. https://doi.org/10.3389%2Ffpsyg.2022.805748.

Kumar, Amit. "Kindness Can Have Unexpectedly Positive Consequences." *Scientific American*, December 12, 2022. https://www.scientificamerican.com/article/kindness-can-have-unexpectedly-positive-consequences/.

Lomas, Tim. "Where Does the Word 'Mindfulness' Come From?" *Psychology Today*, March 16, 2016. https://www.psychologytoday.com/us/blog/finding-light-in-the-darkness/201603/where-does-the-word-mindfulness-come.

Marcus Aurelius. *Meditations*. Translated by James Harris. CreateSpace Independent Publishing Platform, 2016.

Motto, Jerome A., and Alan G. Bostrom. "A Randomized Controlled Trial of Postcrisis Suicide Prevention." *Psychiatric Services* 52, no. 6 (2001): 828–833. https://doi.org/10.1176/appi.ps.52.6.828.

Nelson-Coffey, S. Katherine, Ernst T. Bohlmeijer, and Marijike Schotanus-Dijkstra. "Practicing Other-Focused Kindness and Self-Focused Kindness among Those at Risk for Mental Illness: Results of a Randomized Controlled Trial." *Frontiers in Psychology* 12 (2021): 741546. https://doi.org/10.3389%2Ffpsyg.2021.741546.

Nosrat, Samin. *Salt, Fat, Acid, Heat: Mastering the Elements of Good Cooking*. New York: Simon and Schuster, 2017.

Osho. *Intimacy: Trusting Oneself and the Other*. New York: St. Martin's Griffin, 1997.

Psychology Today. "Forgiveness." Accessed May 16, 20204. https://www.psychologytoday.com/us/basics/forgiveness

Rathore, Mrithunjay, Meghnath Verma, Mohit Nirwan, Soumitra Trivedi, and Vikram Pai. "Functional Connectivity of Prefrontal Cortex in Various Meditation Techniques—A Mini-Review." *International Journal of Yoga* 15, no. 3 (2022): 187–194. https://doi.org/10.4103%2Fijoy.ijoy_88_22.

Ricciardi, Emiliano, Giuseppina Rota, Lorenzo Sani, Claudio Gentili, Anna Gaglianese, Maria Guazzelli, and Pietro Pietrini. "How the Brain Heals Emotional Wounds: The Functional Neuroanatomy of Forgiveness." *Frontiers in Human Neuroscience* 7 (2013): 839. https://doi.org/10.3389%2Ffnhum.2013.00839.

Seneca. *On the Shortness of Life: Life Is Long If You Know How to Use It*. Translated by C. D. N. Costa. New York: Penguin Books, 2005.

Thubten, Gelong. *A Handbook for Hard Times—A Monk's Guide to Fearless Living*. London: Yellow Kite, 2004.

www.ingramcontent.com/pod-product-compliance
Lightning Source LLC
Chambersburg PA
CBHW070117080526
44586CB00013B/1316